Digital Currency: An International Legal and Regulatory Compliance Guide

Authored By

Jeffrey H. Matsuura

Enterprise Business Law Group LLC
USA

General:

1. Any dispute or claim arising out of or in connection with this License Agreement or the Work (including non-contractual disputes or claims) will be governed by and construed in accordance with the laws of the U.A.E. as applied in the Emirate of Dubai. Each party agrees that the courts of the Emirate of Dubai shall have exclusive jurisdiction to settle any dispute or claim arising out of or in connection with this License Agreement or the Work (including non-contractual disputes or claims).

2. Your rights under this License Agreement will automatically terminate without notice and without the need for a court order if at any point you breach any terms of this License Agreement. In no event will any delay or failure by Bentham Science Publishers in enforcing your compliance with this License Agreement constitute a waiver of any of its rights.

3. You acknowledge that you have read this License Agreement, and agree to be bound by its terms and conditions. To the extent that any other terms and conditions presented on any website of Bentham Science Publishers conflict with, or are inconsistent with, the terms and conditions set out in this License Agreement, you acknowledge that the terms and conditions set out in this License Agreement shall prevail.

Bentham Science Publishers Ltd.
Executive Suite Y - 2
PO Box 7917, Saif Zone
Sharjah, U.A.E.
subscriptions@benthamscience.org

BENTHAM SCIENCE PUBLISHERS LTD.

© Bentham Science Publishers Ltd - 2016

CONTENTS

Foreword   *i*

Preface   *iii*

CHAPTERS

1.	**Introduction: An Overview of Digital Currency Regulation and its Legal Implications**	3
2.	**Traditional Regulation of Currency**	13
3.	**Impact of Digital Currency on Traditional Currency Regulation**	17
4.	**Digital Currency, The Challenge of Money Laundering, and a New Framework for the Regulation of Currency**	37
5.	**Digital Currency as a Commodity**	45
6.	**Impact of Digital Currency on Commodity Trading and Markets**	59
7.	**Appropriate Regulatory Oversight for Digital Currency as a Commodity**	63
8.	**Overview of Securities Regulation**	65
9.	**Digital Currencies as Securities and Their Impact on Regulation**	67
10.	**Effective Integration of Digital Currencies and Traditional Securities Regulation**	71
11.	**Regulation of Digital Currency Businesses and Platforms**	77
	References	103
	Subject Index	113

FOREWORD

The key message presented by this book is that there is already a global, comprehensive, and complex framework of laws and regulations applicable to the creation, distribution, and use of digital currencies in effect at the present time. Many of the current headlines associated with virtual currencies around the world emphasize news as to new forms of regulatory oversight specifically directed toward those currencies which are emerging today. This book reminds us that although those newly emerging requirements will be important for the future of virtual currencies, an extremely wide range of laws and regulations are already applicable to those currencies. This book emphasizes the fact that participants in the digital currency economy are presently operating under substantial legal compliance obligations, despite the fact that many of those participants are not even aware of those obligations.

This book is accordingly both a primer on critical legal issues facing the virtual currency community around the world and a compliance guide, assisting that community to plan and launch their activities in a manner which reduces their risk of liability and loss. Readers of this book will learn that the need for legal compliance policies, practices, and procedures in the virtual currency community is not a challenge for the future, but is instead a fundamental requirement of today. Current initiatives to extend and diversify use of digital currencies and their associated computing platforms now operate under an expansive and complex framework of existing laws and regulations. The compliance challenges associated with that environment are numerous, complicated, and immediate. This book makes a significant and timely contribution to those compliance efforts. It provides a special resource for the virtual currency community around the world. Perhaps most important, this book underscores the critical message to the digital currency community that legal compliance is a current obligation, not an issue for the future.

Craig Blakeley
Alliance Law Group LLC
Global Information Technology Law
Brill Research Perspectives in International Information and Communications Technology Law
USA

PREFACE

The dramatic growth in recognition and popularity of Bitcoin in recent years has spurred substantial attention to the range of potential uses for digital currencies of all forms. That attention has led to growing discussion of the legal, regulatory, and public policy issues associated with widespread use of virtual currencies. This book is intended to provide guidance for all parties involved with or interested in development and use of digital currencies. It is written to provide concise and readily accessible information regarding key legal and regulatory compliance issues and obligations associated with activities and operations involving digital currencies. The book is also intended to emphasize the key message that the challenge of effective legal compliance is a critical current issue for the digital currency community, it is not a topic that can be deferred for future consideration.

There is currently substantial discussion of the need for legal and regulatory oversight of virtual currencies. Much of that discussion seems to be presented in the context of creation of new laws. In fact however, virtual currencies are already within the scope of an extensive network of rules and regulations. Even without implementation of new requirements specifically directed toward digital currencies, a wide range of existing laws, regulations, and policies are already applicable to these currencies, and those legal provisions will have a profound impact on the growth of digital currency use. This book helps readers to identify and begin to address their existing legal compliance obligations.

The scope of this book is global. It discusses compliance issues and obligations as they currently exist and as they are emerging in countries around the world. Participants in the virtual currency ecosystem already face legal compliance obligations associated with a wide range of subjects including contract law, taxes, consumer rights, securities law, debtor/creditor relations, criminal law and a variety of other topics. This book is intended to help all parties interested in virtual currency around the world to recognize critical legal issues and to begin to develop and implement their legal compliance strategies. The material presented in this book does not constitute formal legal counsel. All readers must seek appropriate legal advice from their own attorneys who are familiar with their specific needs and situation. The information provided in this book is offered only for informational and educational purposes. Additionally, the author is not aware of any conflicts of interest associated with this book or its contents.

This book provides participants in the virtual currency community, government officials, scholars, and the general public with a resource to help them identify key legal compliance issues associated with digital currency use. With that knowledge, readers can effectively assess the opportunities and challenges offered by virtual currency. They can also begin to understand legal rights and compliance obligations relevant to their own current and future use of digital currency systems.

All participants in the virtual currency community are already operating within the reach of an extensive, diverse, and complex set of legal requirements enforced by multiple jurisdictions. Compliance with those obligations is mandatory, not optional. This book is intended to provide a starting point for individuals and organizations as they assess the extent of their legal compliance obligations and they begin to implement effective strategies to ensure that they successfully and promptly meet those obligations. This book will help readers to begin the process of legal compliance, but we must all recognize that the legal compliance effort is both complicated and perpetual.

Jeffrey H. Matsuura
Enterprise Business Law Group LLC
USA

2

CHAPTER 1

Introduction: An Overview of Digital Currency Regulation and its Legal Implications

Abstract: Digital currency systems make use of cryptographically secure distributed computing networks to exchange economic value and support a growing array of applications. The nature of these computing platforms and the scope of their applications raise important legal compliance issues. Many jurisdictions around the world are examining the extent to which digital currency systems are affected by existing laws and regulations, and the extent to which those existing laws should be modified or new laws enacted to address the growth of digital currencies. It is already clear, however, that a variety of laws and regulation in virtually every jurisdiction are already applicable to digital currency and its applications. In this environment, developers, distributors, and users of digital currency and associated systems already face substantial legal compliance issues. Understanding these current and potential legal compliance requirements is essential for successful use of digital currency platforms and their applications.

Keywords: Bitcoin, blockchain, Brazil, China, consumer protection, conversion, digital currency, public key, laws, mining, money laundering, regulation, wallet.

Led by Bitcoin a range of computer-generated economic value exchange platforms known as digital currency now provide an efficient and transparent mechanism for rapid, convenient, global payments and value exchange transactions. Digital currencies make use of an entirely computer-based system for creating and sharing economic value. In this way, they enable groups of individuals and private organizations to participate directly in economic transactions, without the need for many traditional financial intermediaries, such as banks. This process of financial "disintermediation" facilitated by digital currency has profound legal, regulatory, and public policy implications.

Digital currencies, often also characterized as virtual currencies, are based upon mathematical algorithms. Those algorithms are at the heart of the currencies and they are incorporated into open source software that is accessible to all participants in the digital currency community. Critical activities in the digital currency system such as currency creation and transaction validation are conducted, in effect, through the process of developing solutions for increasingly complex mathematical puzzles. In the Bitcoin network, for example, users download free software, the Bitcoin client software, which they install on their computers. The Bitcoin client software functions as a "wallet" or storage system for bitcoins, and it provides the encryption and digital signature capabilities necessary for participation in the Bitcoin system.

Cryptographically-based secure virtual currency platforms such as Bitcoin are entirely dependent on a public-private encryption key system. That encryption and verification capability is also incorporated into the client software users install on their computers. For Bitcoin, the public keys generated for members of the community consist of alphanumeric strings of characters that are generally between 24 and 37 characters in length. Bitcoin private keys are also randomly generated alphanumeric character strings which are 64 characters in length. Users can create multiple public keys, and for each public key a single, corresponding private key is also created. The public keys are readily accessible to other system users. They serve, in effect, as the identifiable digital currency accounts for users. Each private key is mathematically associated with a single public key. Private keys are not accessible to any party other than the account owner. Private keys are essential for the verification of account owner identity necessary before a digital currency transaction can occur. The private keys essentially serve as the digital currency because access to those keys provides access to all of the currency associated with that particular user account.

Using the downloaded client software, a Bitcoin user must identify the amount to be transferred and the identity of the payment recipient. The user must also verify his or her identity and authorize the transaction through use of a digital signature. All of these steps necessary to execute transactions that are processed by the client software. The user's private key is necessary in order to access the secure wallet in which the user's bitcoins are stored. Use of the private key provides the digital signature necessary to authorize the transaction. In virtual currency systems, security of the private keys is vital as they are the method through which user identity is verified and all transactions are authorized. A party in possession of the private key associated with a digital currency account has complete control over that account.

Bitcoin and other distributed cryptographically-based virtual currency platforms make use of a "blockchain" ledger to document and confirm all transactions. In effect, the blockchain is the record documenting every transaction involving the digital currency. The transaction record, or ledger, contained in the blockchain is complete, unalterable, and accessible to all users of the platform. It provides a complete historical record, in chronological order, of the parties involved in each transactions, the amount of digital currency processed in each transaction, and the time and date of each transaction. The information contained in the blockchain is used to process all transactions and to ensure the continued integrity of the currency system. That integrity is essential in order to preserve the user confidence necessary to keep the system operating as a viable medium of economic value exchange.

Each time that a digital currency transaction is authorized, the details of that transaction are announced to the blockchain. The details associated with each transaction include the public address of the previous owner of the currency now being transferred (*i.e.*, the public address of the party who transferred the currency to the current owner who is now authorizing the current transaction), the amount of currency now being sent, and the proposed recipient's public address. After this transaction information is released to the blockchain, the transaction remains pending for a brief period of time as the blockchain processes the transaction information and ultimately confirms the transaction. For Bitcoin transactions, it generally only takes a few minutes for the confirmation to be received. Transaction confirmation is, in effect, the process through which participants in the network verify mathematically that the currency involved in the proposed transaction is, in fact, owned by the party requesting the transaction and has not previously been transferred to another party.

Blockchain confirmation of each transaction is conducted by the "miners" associated with the blockchain. Miners in the Bitcoin network are the computers that provide the computing capacity to store and support the blockchain. Using the information provided in association with each proposed transaction, the miners use an automated process to review the historical data stored in the blockchain to confirm that the proposed transaction is legitimate and can be accepted by the blockchain. Upon completion of that review, the transaction is confirmed, the transfer of the currency is executed, and the historical record contained in the blockchain ledger is adjusted to reflect the details of the new transaction. Miners receive payment in bitcoin, a transaction fee, for their assistance in confirming all bitcoin transactions.

In addition to reviewing and confirming transactions, miners in the Bitcoin system are responsible for the continuing creation of new bitcoins. Mining is thus the core of the crypto-currency process. It ensures the accuracy and legitimacy of the entire virtual currency platform and community. Mining is conducted through use of software designed for that purpose which is resident on certain computers (nodes) in the virtual currency network. The software is used to solve complex algorithms. In effect, the computers serving as nodes in the digital currency platform have been donated to provide the computing power necessary to provide the verification, analytical, and storage functions necessary to create, support, and maintain the blockchains. In exchange for providing those essential services to the virtual currency community, the miners are granted ownership of some of the newly created digital currency.

In the Bitcoin network, new currency is released subject to a continuing and pre-set schedule [1]. The release of the new bitcoins is reportedly handled through a specific algorithm which provides for release of fifty new bitcoins every ten minutes, with that release rate to be halved approximately every four years until 2140. The Bitcoin system is designed to support creation of a maximum of 21 million bitcoins and when that amount is reached, no new bitcoins will be created. Miners compete to identify the next block of bitcoins. They do this by solving increasingly complex cryptographic puzzles, applying specialized algorithms to massive volumes of data to identify unique patterns associated with the new bitcoin blocks. The first miner to solve the puzzle and identify the new bitcoin block announces the establishment of the new block to the community. After verification of the accuracy of the announced result, the new block is added to the blockchain and the miner involved receives payment of a pre-set amount of the new bitcoins.

The Bitcoin platform and other virtual currencies were originally focused on direct interaction with end users. Under this model, the individuals who intend to spend and otherwise use the virtual currency download the necessary client software directly and establish and manage their own wallets on computer in their possession. Increasingly however, in an effort to appeal to a broader universe of potential digital currency users, third party service providers began to operate, providing services to digital currency users that make use of digital currency more convenient and secure.

Entire ecosystems emerged in association with virtual currency systems such as Bitcoin [2]. At the center of these digital currency platforms are the inventors who create the algorithms and basic software that enable the currencies. Issuers are the parties who generate the currencies and miners make computing resources that they control available for use supporting, validating, and documenting all of the virtual currency transactions. Processing service providers support and facilitate transfer of digital currency units. Storage or wallet service providers enable parties to retain their digital currency holdings. Exchanges and trading platforms provide forums in which digital currencies can be bought and sold. Conversion service providers facilitate the transformation of traditional currencies into digital currencies and *vice versa*. Finally, individuals and businesses willing to accept payment in virtual currency form serve as critical members of the digital currency ecosystems.

Digital currencies are increasingly accepted for use to purchase a range of goods and services. This growing popularity has led notable numbers of people around the world to explore the potential uses of virtual currency for a variety of applications. Although still far from being commonly used in commerce, digital currencies, particularly Bitcoin, are in wide enough use to attract the attention of major businesses and governments in many different parts of the world. Despite the fact that Bitcoin is the most prominent digital currency system in the world, it is not the only such system in operation. A variety of other virtual currency platforms are in operation, including systems such as Litecoin [3].

A diverse variety of nations and regional jurisdictions around the world are beginning to address the public policy, legal, and regulatory implications of the growing popularity and rapidly expanding use of digital currency systems. Some jurisdictions, such as the Channel Islands (Alderney) are reportedly considering policy initiatives to encourage use of digital currencies and to attract commercial operations involving digital currency platforms [4]. Other countries, Belgium for example, remain wary of digital currency systems but see no immediate need to assert active regulatory oversight as to their development and activities [5]. It appears that, at present, a majority of governments around the world have adopted a wait and see posture similar to that of Belgium. This wait and see posture by governments seems to be driven in large measure by the inability of those governments to apply direct control to virtual currency creation and use. Digital currency platforms such as Bitcoin are private systems that operate based on mutual agreement and consent of the participating parties. It is extremely difficult for governments to exercise control over these private systems.

Some authorities are modifying their legal and regulatory frameworks in an effort to accommodate development of digital currency platforms. This type of effort is underway in Brazil, for instance. In 2013, the Brazilian government enacted legislation that paved the way for expanded use of digital currencies and other forms of electronic and mobile payments [6]. The legislation granted authority for the creation of electronic currencies and it defined electronic currencies as resources that are stored on a device or on an electronic system which enable end users to perform a payment activity. The law and associated authorization apply to digital currencies such as Bitcoin and to a wide range of other electronic and mobile payment platforms.

The Brazilian legislative initiative is significant for several different reasons. It is important as it reflects a belief on the part of Brazilian authorities that enabling legislation is helpful to clarify and manage the growing public interest in digital currency use. Many other jurisdictions, perhaps the majority of them, have not yet concluded that broad legislative action is needed during the early stages of digital currency development. Most governments seem, at present, to adopt a strategy that permits and monitors digital currency development without creation of a formal legal and regulatory oversight structure.

Brazil's digital currency legislation is also noteworthy for its definition of electronic currency. The Brazilian law adopts a seemingly broad definition of digital currency giving the law substantial potential reach. Brazil has defined digital currency in a manner which includes crypto-currency systems such as Bitcoin and the current range of digital currency platforms. In addition, the Brazilian law also includes in the category of electronic currency essentially all payment systems that make use of digital communications and information processing devices and networks. The scope of applicability for the Brazilian law is extensive. The government of Brazil has essentially classified a very wide range of electronic payment systems as electronic currency. This expansive approach to digital currency oversight can have significant future impact.

The Brazilian approach addresses legal, regulatory, and public policy issues associated with virtual currencies within the broader context of electronic payment platforms and mechanisms in general. There seems to be substantial merit to this strategy. It seems more efficient and effective to examine the full range of electronic payments systems together, instead of attempting to distinguish digital currencies from other existing and emerging digital payment systems. Instead of considering the need for legal oversight specifically directed toward digital currencies, it is more sensible to examine virtual currency in the context of the growing and diversifying set of electronic payment options. The appropriate goal for governments should be facilitating development of a suite of electronic payment platform options which is convenient for users, yet also secure and efficient.

A minority of jurisdictions have elected to prohibit or severely limit the use of digital currencies. In some instances the stated reasons for the prohibitions seem to include concerns such as the volatility of digital currency valuations, the likelihood of user confusion, and the potential for money laundering activities. In some jurisdictions, there is also concern as to the security of the virtual currency system. It is also likely, however, that governments that restrict digital currency use may also fear loss of control over financial transactions and commercial relationships. To the extent that virtual currency platforms such as Bitcoin provide users with the opportunity to participate directly in the creation and operation of the value exchange system, and they provide a transparent system to support all transactions, the virtual currency communities have the potential to empower individuals. Such empowerment can create challenges for governments that rely on extensive control over their citizens.

An example of a government which at present severely restricts digital currency use is the government of China. Chinese authorities characterize Bitcoin and other digital currencies as "virtual commodities" instead of currency [7]. In China, banks and other payment institutions are prohibited from dealing in Bitcoin and other digital currencies. They are prohibited from buying or selling the digital currencies. They are also barred from accepting or using digital currencies as payment for goods or services. Banks and payment institutions in China are also prohibited from converting Bitcoin and other digital currencies to traditional currencies. This regulatory approach in China illustrates a form of indirect regulation available to governments. Instead of directly banning creation, distribution, and use of virtual currencies, some governments elect to prohibit use or acceptance of those currencies by key regulated institutions, such as banks and other financial service providers. In this way, development and use of virtual currencies is limited without the need for regulatory action to ban the digital currencies.

At present, the most active approach to legal and regulatory oversight of virtual currency operations involves application of laws and rules governing the transmission of money. These laws are in place in virtually every jurisdiction in the world, and they have as their primary focus prevention of money laundering, the conversion of funds obtained through illegal conduct into legitimate commercial activities. Legal requirements designed to block money laundering are, at present, the most popular vehicles applied by government to monitor and influence virtual currency systems and transactions. These laws tend to focus on registration, monitoring, and reporting requirements for all parties engaged in money transmission. A rapidly growing number of jurisdictions now apply rules governing money transmission to key participants in the virtual currency ecosystem, such as currency exchanges and conversion service providers.

Another highly active existing framework of laws now routinely applied to influence digital currency activities is the set of rules that govern the offering of financial services. In many jurisdictions, banking, commodities trading, foreign exchange conversion, and a variety of other financial services are regulated by government authorities. Numerous jurisdictions around the world now interpret those rules to apply to specific aspect of the virtual currency marketplace, such as the conversions between digital currencies and the traditional national currencies such as the dollar and the euro. A rapidly growing number of governments now routinely characterize critical digital currency operations as regulated financial services, and thus subject those operations to the existing financial regulatory structure.

The digital currency community also operates under a complex set of contractual arrangements connecting virtually all key participants in that community. Parties who create, share, store, and use virtual currencies conduct essentially all of their activities subject to contracts. The terms and conditions established in those agreements set the boundaries and expectations of the digital currency marketplace. Contract law thus already plays a critical role in the creation, distribution, and use of all forms of digital currency. The terms of those agreements, the negotiation processes that establish the agreements, and the mechanisms through which digital currency contract disputes are resolved comprise a critical set of legal compliance issues now facing the virtual currency sector in all parts of the world.

In the very near future, other existing legal requirements will almost certainly be directed aggressively toward the virtual currency ecosystem. For example, it is increasingly clear that the full range of consumer protection standards and regulations will be applied to digital currency transactions, relationships, and services. As Bitcoin and other digital currency systems grow in reach and popularity, consumer protection laws and regulations will certainly be engaged actively in the virtual currency environment. Additionally, the extensive global framework of criminal laws against misuse of computers, computer networks, and the data processed on computer systems will likely be applied actively in the context of virtual currency systems, transactions, and operations. Given the broad reach of computer and data crime laws around the world, a wide range of activities involving digital currency networks will likely to be viewed to be within the scope of those laws in the near future.

When considering the legal, regulatory, and public policy compliance issues associated with the world of virtual currency, it is important to recognize two key facets of those issues. One set of legal concerns exists with regard to the development and operation of the technologies, systems, and platforms that enable, support, and sustain virtual currencies and their associated applications. Another set of legal concerns is present with respect to the interaction of the diverse virtual currency applications with individual consumers and with businesses and organizations operating outside of the virtual currency community.

Generally, it is the goal of a legal system to provide fair and consistent oversight. Rules should be transparent and applied in the same manner to all parties who are in the same, or similar, situations. Perhaps the most important challenge that virtual currency platforms and their applications present for legal systems around the world is the wide range of uses and applications they can support. Those platforms can process payments for transactions, support creation and trading of securities and other financial instruments, facilitate the negotiation, execution, and enforcement of commercial contracts, and support an ever-expanding array of other diverse activities.

Given this wide range of applications, there is not currently and there never will be a single set of law, regulations or rules governing all of the activities of digital currency platforms. There will never be a true "digital currency law." Instead, expansion of the activities of virtual currency platforms will have an impact on nearly every existing category of law. Digital currency will impact the law of contracts and commercial transactions, consumer protection law, securities law, property law, the law of trusts and estates, and essentially every other class of law and regulation. This condition is not novel. We have seen the same evolution as the Internet developed and expanded, and as the scope and sophistication of electronic commerce blossomed. With both the Internet in general and e-commerce in particular, dramatic expansion in scope of use led to application of virtually all forms of law and regulation to the activities, transactions, and relationships associated with the Internet and with e-commerce. A similar progression will develop with virtual currency platform use. As the scope and diversity of applications for the virtual currency platforms expand, a growing array of laws and regulations will come into play in association with those platforms.

In this setting, an incredibly large and complex set of legal compliance challenges are already present for everyone participating in the virtual currency marketplace.

Although there are currently relatively few laws specifically directed toward digital currencies and their use, an extensive set of existing laws in all jurisdictions have the potential to affect digital currency development and use. Legal compliance for the virtual currency community is already a major concern. This book will help to identify the nature and scope of legal compliance demands now facing the digital currency community.

CHAPTER 2

Traditional Regulation of Currency

Abstract: National governments apply well-established rules addressing the creation and use of fiat currency used in their countries. Fiat currency is often also described as a nation's legal tender. It is the national currency, issued and guaranteed by the national government. At present, no nation has established any form of digital currency as its sole form of fiat currency. For this reason, traditional laws governing currency have not been directly applicable to Bitcoin and other virtual currencies.

Keywords: Bank, currency, digital currency, fiat currency, fiduciary currency, laws, legal tender, New Zealand, private money, regulations, Turkey, virtual currency.

Legal currency is widely recognized to consist of money which a national government requires that all parties accept to satisfy all debts and other financial obligations. Sometimes described as, "legal tender", official currency can only be authorized and created by a national government. In many countries, national law requires that official currency can only be issued by the national bank. It is important to recognize that in virtually all economies, a wide range of mechanisms and services are routinely used to transfer economic value from one party to another. In general however, the only form of value exchange which can be offered by all parties to satisfy a financial obligation is legal currency. The official currency of a country is sometimes characterized as the nation's "fiat currency."

The critical aspect of national fiat currency is government backing. National governments guarantee the integrity of their currency. Although they can not assure their citizens of a specific level of value for the national currency, governments do guarantee to their citizens that they provide full backing for the national currency, and that they oversee the creation and use of the currency. Individuals have faith in the integrity of national currency to the extent that they have faith in their government.

Although currency can be offered to satisfy all debts and charges, in the United States and other jurisdictions parties are not required to accept currency as satisfaction for amounts owed [8]. A business can, for example, require payments using checks or other value exchange mechanisms in lieu of currency. The legal status of currency simply establishes currency as the value exchange system which can be offered to satisfy all financial obligations. Legal tender carries a government guarantee of value which distinguishes it from other forms of payment established by agreement among private parties.

Some governments apply a narrow definition of currency. They focus on the physical and tangible nature of notes and coins. For example, the Reserve Bank of New Zealand noted that it focuses its attention to on circulating currency. Accordingly, the Reserve Bank of New Zealand indicated that creation and use of Bitcoin and other virtual currencies by parties other than banks does not fall within the Bank's jurisdiction and such action does not require approval from the Bank [9]. New Zealand currency authorities take the position that their jurisdiction reaches only to the tangible notes and coins that are backed by the New Zealand government. Private forms of money and economic value exchange presented in electronic form are not within the scope of the Reserve Bank's oversight authority.

Even those jurisdictions that have adopted a legal framework directly applicable to electronic money do not necessarily apply that framework to digital currencies. For instance, in Turkey, the Banking Regulation and Supervision Agency determined that Bitcoin is not electronic money, and is thus not subject to the terms of Turkey's Law on Payment and Securities Reconciliation [10]. In jurisdictions such as Turkey, the determination that virtual currencies do not constitute a form of electronic money takes those currencies out of the scope of coverage of rules directed toward electronic money and payments.

Many different methods for transferring economic value, in addition to formal legal currency are available. For example, checks and other financial instruments can be used to transfer value between two parties willing to offer and accept such non-currency transfers. Transfers of legal tender are not the only method to make payments or to satisfy financial obligations. Parties can use a wide range of alternatives to currency for transfer of economic value. Debts can be satisfied and payments can be made using virtually any medium of value exchange acceptable to all of the parties involved.

Over time, the concept of fiduciary currency has emerged. Fiduciary currency is not an official national fiat currency authorized and support by government, but is instead a medium for exchange of economic value that derives its value based solely on the willingness of users to accept it [11]. Fiduciary currency derives its value entirely from the trust and agreement of the parties who use it. Viewed from this perspective, successful virtual currencies can be reasonably recognized as forms of fiduciary currency. Another description of this type of value exchange medium is, private money.

Systems of private money operate outside of the scope of traditional national currencies. Private money systems do not have governments or any other single party functioning as guarantors of the value of the private currency. Instead, each party to the transactions involving the private currency assumes all risks associated with the currency. The only economic value associated with the currency arises from the willingness of individual parties to accept the currency in exchange for goods and services. The greater that acceptance, the more valuable is the currency. Private money systems can, accordingly, be highly volatile. Events or conditions that undermine user faith in the value of the currency can dramatically affect the utility of the currency. The vast majority of governments around the world recognize that Bitcoin and other digital currencies are, in effect, private money systems.

Matsuura Chapter 3:
Impact of Digital Currency on Traditional Currency Regulation

CHAPTER 3

Impact of Digital Currency on Traditional Currency Regulation

Abstract: National authorities regulating currency generally do not have direct jurisdiction over virtual currencies, to date, as they are not national fiat currencies. However, currency regulators are influencing development of digital currency in several key indirect ways. Through their authority to protect the value and integrity of national fiat currencies, they take actions affecting digital currencies claiming that such actions are necessary to protect their national currency. Additionally, as these regulators generally have the authority to control the activities of banks and other key financial institutions, they influence digital currency development and use by restricting the ability of those institutions to use or accept virtual currency. Currency regulators commonly have jurisdiction over conversion of foreign currency, and through this role, they now routinely restrict the ability of parties to conduct conversions between digital currencies and traditional national currencies. National currency regulators have also issued substantial warnings to consumers of the risks associated with digital currency use. Currency regulators often have authority over funds transmission and money transfers, and they frequently exercise that jurisdiction in the context of virtual currency use. Some government are now exploring the possibility of government controlled digital currency and of government participation in the blockchain of existing virtual currency platforms.

Keywords: Banks, Bolivia, Brazil, Canada, China, consumer protection, Croatia, currency, currency conversion, Cyprus, digital currency, Ecuador, Electronic Currency System, European Union, fiat currency, financial institutions, financial services, foreign exchange, France, Germany, government participation, Iceland, India, Indonesia, Isle of Man, itBit, Kenya, Kyrgyzstan, legal tender, Luxembourg, Malta, Mexico, money transfer, M-Pesa, national currency, Netherlands, New York, Nigeria, private money, Russia, Singapore, Thailand, units of account, Vietnam, wallet.

Digital currency platforms can be created and operated by private organizations and by groups of individuals. Governments are not required, from an operational perspective, to develop or operate digital currency systems. As a result, digital currencies emerge and evolve beyond the control of governments. In effect, today's existing virtual currency systems are best characterized as private money platforms. They provide effective mediums of exchange only to the extent that a critical mass of willing users exists. Without that universe of willing users, private money has no value. The economic value of virtual currency systems, and thus their effectiveness as a commercial mechanism, is entirely dependent on the

Jeffrey H. Matsuura
All rights reserved-© 2016 Bentham Science Publishers

existence of a pool of willing users who accept the currencies in exchange for goods and services.

To date, no country has established digital currency as legal tender. This means that digital currency is not a formal national currency in any jurisdiction. Although bitcoin and other forms of digital currency are in wide use around the world, they do not constitute legal tender. The value of digital currency is based on the willingness of the parties to a financial transaction to offer and accept the digital exchange as a valid transfer of economic value. Digital currencies are not supported or guaranteed by any government. Accordingly, they inevitably carry greater risk for users than traditional currencies.

As digital currencies are not created through authorization or action by governments, they are not legal tender and are accordingly not subject to regulatory oversight as formal currency. Despite this status, some jurisdictions authorize the regulatory authorities that oversee traditional currency to play a role in oversight of digital currencies. In many countries the lead regulatory authority overseeing currency creation and use is the nation's central bank or its finance ministry. To date, that role has primarily involved informing the public as to what digital currencies are and how they are used. Additionally, currency regulators in many different parts of the world have been active cautioning the public with regard to the risks associated with digital currency use. To be clear, however, because digital currencies are not true currency, the actual authority of national banks and other currency regulators around the world to regulate digital currencies directly is extremely limited.

It is important to note that government can have a significant impact on the development of virtual currency systems without exerting direct regulatory oversight. Governments can make use of digital currencies without designating them as legal tender. Numerous governments in different parts of the world, for example, now accept bitcoin as payment for fees and other amounts owed by businesses and individuals. Acceptance of digital currencies by governments to satisfy financial obligations does not constitute designation of those digital currencies as formal legal tender. Government acceptance does, however, provide users of the currencies with substantially greater confidence in the utility of the currencies and thus helps to maintain or increase their value. By acting as users of digital currencies, governments can promote digital currency development and can influence key aspects of that development. In a practical sense, governments may be able to have greater and more immediate impact on virtual currency use by participating in the digital currency economy than by attempting to develop and apply traditional forms of regulatory oversight.

No government has chosen to treat digital currency as a traditional form of currency for regulatory purposes. For example, Canada's Department of Finance specifically determined that digital currency is not legal tender and is thus not subject to traditional currency oversight and controls [12]. This approach is sensible. Currency supported by the traditional designation of legal tender can only be created under government authorization. No digital currency has yet received such authorization. Accordingly, no digital currency should yet be subjected to traditional currency oversight.

Authorities in the Netherlands also take the position that digital currencies do not constitute formal currency [13]. The Dutch authorities take this position as digital currencies are not issued in exchange for money and they do not represent binding claims against the parties who issue the currency. Under Dutch law, formal currency must be issued in exchange for money and must generate a legally enforceable claim against the issuer of the currency.

The central bank of France, the Banque de France, does not consider virtual currency to be an official currency or a formal means of payment. Instead the French central bank views digital currency to be a form of payment service. As such, the French central bank suggests that virtual currency processing should be handled only by authorized payment service providers that are subject to the existing licensing and operating rules of the French Prudential Supervisory Authority [14]. The French approach seems to treat virtual currency as a service instead of as a formal currency or an asset or a form of property. This is an increasingly popular strategy for governments. Instead of extending the reach of currency regulations to apply to digital currencies, a growing number of governments now choose to define digital currency operations as financial services and thus subject those operations to existing rules and regulations applicable to the provision of financial services.

Authorities in Indonesia also indicated their interpretation that virtual currencies are not official currency. Bank Indonesia, the Indonesian central bank, advised the public that bitcoin and other forms of virtual currency are not official currency [15]. Accordingly, they are not guaranteed by the government and users of the digital currencies bear all risks associated with such use. The efforts by Bank Indonesia to warn the public as to potential digital currency risks and to provide information on those currencies to citizens are illustrative of similar efforts now in progress in many other countries.

Singapore's Inland Revenue Authority also concluded that Bitcoin and other forms of digital currency do not constitute official currency [16]. Although virtual currency can provide a useful means for exchange of economic value between willing parties, the Inland Revenue Authority noted that digital currencies do not have official government authorization and do not have the status of currency. Governments around the world seem to believe that the key message to be presented to their citizens is that digital currencies are not backed by the government and are thus highly volatile and carry greater risk of loss than traditional national currency.

The government of Ecuador has launched an extensive electronic payment system which has been characterized as digital currency, however, that description does not seem to be entirely accurate. Ecuador operates using the United States dollar as the nation's currency. The Ecuadoran government launched its "Sistema de Dinero Eletronico" in late 2014 [17]. That system provides for widespread electronic payments, however, all such payments are made in dollars, not using the token-based system of Bitcoin and other digital currencies. In fact, all other forms of virtual currency are prohibited in Ecuador, providing the government-operated electronic payment system an effective monopoly on electronic payments made in the country.

As the Ecuadoran system is based on the dollar, it appears to be a classic electronic payment system instead of a true digital currency platform. The fiat currency in Ecuador continues to be the dollar, however, the new system supports and encourages broader use of electronic payments. Instead of creating a new digital currency, the government of Ecuador seems to have implemented a government-operated national electronic payment processing platform. Ecuadoran authorities characterize the new system as the "Electronic Currency System" and they require that all banks in the country integrate their operations into the new system by the middle of 2016 [18].

The Ecuadoran system does not truly constitute a national virtual currency system, but is instead a supplement to the existing dollar-based national currency framework. Indeed, it can be argued that, because the country currently prohibits use of private digital currency systems, Ecuador has effectively blocked the development of a true virtual currency platform. That barrier appears to be even more complete as the Ecuadoran government has reportedly taken legislative action to ban all virtual currency systems other than the one launched by the government [19]. In effect, the government of Ecuador seems to be creating a government-based virtual currency platform which will replace all other digital currencies, but the government-mandated digital currency is actually the dollar, thus the country's proposed electronic currency seems instead to be simply a nation-wide electronic payment system.

It is unclear what the legal basis for banning other virtual currency platforms in Ecuador would be. To the extent that all digital currency systems that are not government-backed are private value exchange platforms, most governments take the position that they do not have the authority to prohibit such collaborative networks that are based upon the mutual agreement of all the participants. By banning private virtual currency systems, the government of Ecuador guarantees a greater level of usage for the government-run platform, however, that approach also prevents user choice and denies access to other commercial applications now available on Bitcoin and other private digital currency platforms.

Other nations are actively considering possible methods to integrate virtual currency platforms into their national currency structures. For example, the Mexican government is evaluating potential digital currency use in support of the peso. At present that planning remains in its early stages and the framework under discussion would involve government participation in digital currency "block chain" systems [20]. Under this approach, the Mexican government would be an active participant in an existing virtual currency platform and would integrate that digital currency system into its peso-based national currency structure. Presumably, if the Mexican government elected to participate in the block chain of an existing digital currency platform, such as Bitcoin, instead of establishing its own proprietary platform as the government of Ecuador seems to have done, government entry into the digital currency ecosystem could occur much more quickly and efficiently.

If a national government ever chose to establish its currency in digital format, then presumably that digital currency would be subject to all of the same oversight and regulatory controls that have long been applied to traditional currency. Restrictions on creation, distribution, and use of digital currency would most likely parallel those applicable to tangible currency. It remains unclear how such a structure would be applied in a virtual currency platform environment. For example, if a government-backed digital currency was to function as a nation's true fiat currency, then the laws in most nations would require that only the national government could issue that currency, presumably meaning that only the government could operate and manage the virtual currency platform. Additionally, there would likely be important questions regarding the interplay between digital and tangible versions of the national currency.

For the present, the phrase, "digital currency" is somewhat misleading. The digital value exchange mechanisms now in operation, including perhaps the most popular of those mechanisms, Bitcoin, are not really forms of currency, as they have not been so designated by any national government. Perhaps a more accurate characterization of today's digital currencies is as digital value exchange platforms. Instead of operating as forms of currency authorized and regulated by governments, today's digital currencies are privately established, operated, and managed electronic systems that enable willing users to create and share economic value. Formal currency is created and backed by national governments, digital currencies are established through agreements among private parties.

Even the digital currency initiative underway in Ecuador falls short of a true virtual currency model. Ecuador's digital currency program is an extension of its existing, dollar-based currency system. Each digital dollar in Ecuador is a representation of a tangible dollar. The value of Ecuadoran digital dollars is equal to the value of the tangible dollar. In a true virtual currency system, the digital currency would have independent value set based on supply and demand for the digital currency. The digital value platform in Ecuador extends the dollar-based economy into a national electronic payment system but it does not establish a true digital currency.

Some national currency authorities have specifically acknowledged that digital currencies are legally binding financial instruments even though they are not formal legal currency. For example, the German Financial Supervisory Authority has opted to treat digital currencies in much the same way that it recognizes the foreign currency of other countries [21]. The German authorities consider foreign currencies to be "units of account" that are legally binding and they are now applying that same conceptual model to bitcoin and other digital currency.

The approach adopted by German financial authorities is applicable to all other currency regulators around the world. In effect, Germany treats digital currencies as foreign currencies, despite the fact that the digital currencies are not formal legal currencies of other countries. This approach is based on recognition that transactions involving the digital currencies are legally binding upon parties who choose to participate in those transactions. The digital currencies represent units of value that private parties agree to accept as enforceable financial instruments. Although digital currencies are not established or controlled by national governments, the German approach provides a model for effective recognition of those digital units of accounts, and for successful integration of digital currencies into the traditional international network of official currencies.

The German strategy of treating digital currencies as foreign currencies takes the regulatory emphasis off of currency oversight and places it instead on the conversion process. Just as no government has the authority to regulate the national currency of another country, the German model makes use of the premise that German currency regulators do not have authority over virtual currencies. German currency regulators do, however, have oversight authority over activities that could undermine the integrity of German currency and over the conversion between German currency and foreign currencies. It is the authority over foreign currency conversion and protection of the integrity of the national currency which provides the basis for limited regulatory oversight over virtual currencies.

Authorities in India also appear to be applying a framework that treats digital currencies as foreign currencies, at least in part, for regulatory purposes. The Reserve Bank of India indicated that Bitcoin and other digital currencies are not true currencies and are thus not within the regulatory oversight of the Bank. The Bank issued a warning to the public about the potential risks associated with digital currency use [22]. Despite this interpretation, regulatory authorities in India reportedly took legal action against a party who hosted Bitcoin operations in India, alleging that the party was operating in violation of India's Foreign Exchange Management Act [23]. Obviously, the regulatory climate for virtual currencies in India remains uncertain, yet it appears that one emerging theme in government review of digital currency operations in India is the interpretation that virtual currency transactions may be analogous to foreign currency transactions.

Croatia also applies a regulatory approach to digital currencies similar to that of Germany. Croatia specifically notes that bitcoin and other digital currencies are not legal tender established by the government, but their commercial use is not illegal [24]. Croatian authorities recognize digital currencies as legal platforms for the exchange of value among private parties. As is the case in Germany, Croatian authorities view digital currencies in a manner similar to foreign currencies. Conceptually, Croatia addresses digital currencies in much the same way that it interacts with national currencies of other countries.

Regulators in Iceland do not consider digital currency to be formal currency, yet they monitor the international trade of digital currencies. The Central Bank of Iceland took the position that digital currencies are subject to existing rules applicable to international trading of those currencies [25]. Iceland's Foreign Exchange Act applies restrictions to the international transfer of currency. Iceland's Central Bank indicated that those limitations on international currency exchange are applicable to digital currencies. Thus although digital currencies are not viewed to be formal currency in Iceland, Icelandic authorities chose to apply the international currency exchange restrictions of Icelandic law to those virtual currencies. Under the Icelandic approach, trading and conversion of virtual currency are viewed to be, in effect, forms of foreign currency transactions subject to regulatory oversight. It is not clear, however, if the basic process of creating (mining) digital currency in Iceland is also subject to that regulatory oversight. One can reasonably argue that mining digital currency is not a transaction, however this interpretation has yet to be resolved.

This illustrates the somewhat confused and at times inconsistent approach to digital currency oversight present in many jurisdictions. It also underscores the increasingly popular approach adopted by regulatory authorities treating digital currencies in a manner similar to that applied to foreign currencies. National banks and other government authorities tasked with the mission of protecting the integrity of national currencies increasingly use that mission as a basis for monitoring and regulating virtual currencies.

In some jurisdictions, the decision to treat virtual currencies in a manner similar to foreign currencies, from a regulatory perspective, results in barriers to digital currency use. It appears that, at present, the most common excuse for prohibiting digital currency use is the contention that such a prohibition is necessary as part of effective oversight of foreign currency exchange and use. Countries that pursue this strategy do not expressly ban virtual currencies, however, they prohibit conversion of the currencies into the national currency or they block the international transfer of the digital currencies. The authorities are thus not specifically banning digital currency use, an action they generally do not have the legal authority to take, but are instead restricting digital currency use through exercise of their authority to control foreign currency trading and conversion.

For example, some observers have noted that the government of Thailand has blocked Bitcoin use in that country [26]. Others correctly recognized that the authorities in Thailand have not totally prohibited use of Bitcoin or other digital currencies [27]. Instead, they presently block trading, conversion, and transfer of Bitcoin and other virtual currencies under their authority to regulate foreign currency exchange activities that affect the value and stability of Thailand's national currency.

In addition to Thailand, other nations that are blocking virtual currency expansion are establishing those barriers through use of the legal and regulatory processes associated with their oversight of the impact of foreign currency on the national currency. For instance, the government of Vietnam currently resists digital currency use through its controls over currency trading. It presently applies those controls to bar trading of electronic currencies [28]. Similarly, the government of Bolivia imposed a ban on digital currency use, justifying that action as a step necessary to protect the public and to preserve the value of the national currency [29]. To the extent that virtual currencies can be used as alternatives to traditional national currencies, even if the virtual currencies are not legally recognized as true currency, the virtual currencies have the potential to affect the value of the traditional currencies. This dynamic essentially assures that any government authority with the job of managing the integrity of a national currency can readily create a justification for regulating or otherwise overseeing digital currency distribution, conversion, and use even without any additional specific legal authorization.

Some governments have moved actively to block and limit development of digital currencies through control over banks and other financial institutions. For example, the government of China treats Bitcoin and other digital currencies as "virtual" commodities and expressly indicates that they are not currency [30]. Chinese authorities prohibit banks and payment processing institutions from making use of Bitcoin and other forms of digital currency. Countries taking this approach are not directly banning use of virtual currencies, but are instead restricting their use by limiting the ability of financial institutions to trade and process those currencies. In these jurisdictions, digital currency is not recognized as currency and its use as a private payment platform is also restricted.

Some jurisdictions are moving toward direct bans on digital currency use. Perhaps the most visible example of this restrictive approach is presented by Russia. It is anticipated that at some point in 2015, Russian authorities will impose a broad ban on virtual currency use [31]. It is expected that the Russian ban will prohibit distribution and use of Bitcoin and all other crypto-currencies. When implemented, this ban will likely be the most extensive national barrier to digital currency use in the world. If enacted as anticipated, this approach could make Russia one of the most inhospitable environments for digital currency in the world. It should be noted that the anticipated Russian ban on crypto-currencies is based in a new legislative initiative, not on application of existing regulatory oversight authority over the Russian national currency.

In addition to Russia, a few other nations are creating regulatory environments that essentially block use of virtual currencies. For example, the National Bank of Kyrgyzstan takes the position that use of digital currencies violates that country's laws establishing national currency [32]. Authorities in Kyrgyzstan seem to consider virtual currencies to be direct threats to the national currency, not as private platforms for value exchange. This interpretation of existing currency laws in Kyrgyzstan effectively blocks development of virtual currency systems in that country.

Other national authorities, while not taking formal action to block or control digital currencies, instead choose to warn the public as to the risks associated with those virtual currencies and to caution private parties as to their potential adverse consequences. An example of this cautionary role by national authorities is provided by the Central Bank of Cyprus which alerted the public that there is no formal government oversight of digital currencies and that their use generally occurs beyond the control of government [33].

It appears that, in those countries where formal action to bar virtual currency use is in progress, the key government concern regarding use of the currency is loss of government control. The distributed structure of virtual currency platforms, and the relative anonymity of their users, make it extremely difficult for governments to assert control over the operations of those platforms. Even if this loss of control does not immediately result in any direct adverse consequences for a nation or its economy, reduction in value of the national currency for instance, there is little doubt that proliferation of virtual currency networks and expansion of their use creates a commercial marketplace that is largely outside of the control of government authorities. In addition, these private platforms are at present also substantially beyond the control of other major national institutions, such as banks. This loss of government influence over economic activity is seriously troubling to many governments around the world and appears to be one of the key reasons why the nations that are acting to block virtual currency development have elected to take that approach.

Although digital currency has not yet attained legal currency status, digital currency is increasingly widely used as a medium of payment. It is widely accepted as a mechanism for the exchange of economic value and is thus an increasingly active participant in the global payment processing network. National governments are not required to grant any form of digital currency true legal tender status, and to date none have done so. The rapidly expanding popularity of digital currency in many different regions of the world does, however, force national governments to develop strategies and policies to accommodate widespread digital currency use. The German conceptual approach of recognizing and accommodating digital currencies in essentially the same manner as that applied to foreign currencies seems sensible and provides a useful and effective model for other governments.

Some authorities are modifying their existing legal and regulatory framework for currency and payment processes in response to the rise of digital currencies and other forms of electronic transactions. For example, as noted previously Brazil enacted national legislation recognizing payment platforms it characterizes as electronic currencies [34]. This classification includes both digital currencies as well as the full range of electronic and mobile payment systems. Brazil's actions on this issue provide a useful illustration of efforts by a government to accommodate and encourage digital currencies and other merging electronic payment platforms.

In addition to the issue of regulatory oversight for digital currency, there is also the issue of regulation of the exchanges that support digital currency trading and conversion of digital currency to traditional currency. It is now increasingly common for jurisdictions to forgo direct regulation of digital currency, while at the same time asserting regulatory oversight as to the exchanges and markets that process trading and currency conversion. For example, authorities in France and Luxembourg do not directly regulate the use of digital currencies however they assert oversight authority as to digital currency exchanges.

Oversight of digital currency trading exchanges is commonly exercised as part of a government's authority to regulate financial services. Countries such as France and Luxembourg regulate financial service offerings, and those nations now include digital currency exchanges and various other digital currency intermediaries as financial service providers [35]. Under this approach, the range of providers of digital currency support services such as storage, trading, and conversions are viewed to be providers of regulated financial services. In many instances, regulators require that parties offering financial services to the public must meet certain requirements such as registration, licensing, and information disclosure. Other jurisdictions do not view virtual currency trading to be a regulated financial service. For instance, Malta determined that digital currencies are not financial instruments and are thus not subject to the licensing requirements of the Malta Financial Services Authority [36].

In addition to the digital currency trading exchanges, there are a number of other parties providing important intermediary services to support digital currency use. For example, processing service providers facilitate the transfer of digital currency units from one party to another. These digital currency processors provide important services to currency users. Other parties provide digital currency storage ("wallet") services. Another critical element of the digital currency ecosystem is the conversion between digital currency and traditional currency. In order to make extensive use of gains realized through digital currency, those holding must be converted into traditional currencies. Authorities such as the Central Bank of France now take the position that digital currency conversion services are payment services that are subject to regulatory oversight [37]. Increasingly, all of these intermediaries are being viewed as financial service providers, and thus subject to existing financial service regulations.

The application of rules governing financial services to the diverse participants in the digital currency system remains uncertain, at present. For example, the European Union regulates both the operation of electronic money services and European payments services [38]. At present however, the EU does not apply either of those sets of rules to digital currency. The provisions overseeing payment services are not designed to address the digital currency platforms that have emerged, and the current digital currency platforms that have developed operate in a manner that falls outside of the scope of the EU's definition of electronic money. For the present, digital currencies are not viewed by the EU to fall within the scope of its oversight of payment services or electronic money.

The regulatory landscape emerging globally seems to exempt digital currency itself from regulatory oversight, yet simultaneously address key intermediary services as regulated financial services. Thus while nation after nation asserts that it will not regulate digital currency, many of those same nations apply their existing financial services regulations to the various key intermediary service providers who make digital currency useful. Jurisdictions around the world at present choose not to regulate the parties who issue digital currencies or the parties who use the currencies in commercial transactions. Instead, regulatory attention is primarily directed toward the diverse intermediary parties who process and support digital currency use. The justification for this assertion of regulatory jurisdiction is that the intermediary services constitute, in effect, financial services offered to the public.

One of the unique aspects of Bitcoin and other virtual currency systems is the fact that individual people and organizations can participate directly in the creation and use of those systems, without relying on use of intermediaries. So for example, an individual can participate in the mining of software and can manage the storage of his or her digital currency holding directly. In most instances, regulation of financial services is applicable only when the parties providing the services are offering those services commercially to third parties. Although the legal and regulatory environment remains unsettled at present, it is likely that even if key functions associated with the creation, distribution and use of virtual currencies are deemed to be regulated financial services in multiple jurisdictions, that regulatory oversight would not be applied in those instances in which individual people or organizations are engaging in the digital currency activities directly and for their own purposes, not as part of commercial service offerings made available to other parties.

The fact that no nation has yet designated any form of digital currency as its official fiat currency does not mean that such action could never be taken. Conceptually, digital currency could serve as a country's official national currency if the citizens and the government involved so chose. It seems most likely that the countries most receptive to consideration of this strategy will be those where the public does not have a great deal of confidence in the stability and reliability of the currency as a medium of exchange and where the value of the currency is highly volatile.

In countries where the official currency is subject to volatile valuation, individuals and businesses may prefer to use Bitcoin and other virtual currencies as the vehicle for storing economic value. People want to hold their economic assets in forms that protect the value of those assets. If the national currency is subject to rapid devaluation, citizens and businesses can lose substantial value quickly. In this type of environment, they may prefer to hold digital currency if the digital currency provides more stable valuation.

To be attractive as an alternative to an established currency, virtual currencies must be widely accepted and readily convertible. Only if digital currency can be used for a wide variety of transactions will it be actively embraced by businesses and individuals. Additionally, a virtual currency must be easy to convert to traditional currencies. Without such ready conversions, people and businesses will be reluctant to hold digital currencies. A key element of the value of a virtual currency is its ready convertibility to both the fiat currency of the home nation and to the currencies of other countries. Some economists suggest that a notable part of the potential value and attractiveness of virtual currency is its convertibility to foreign currency.

Numerous groups are in the process of developing digital currency conversion services to facilitate rapid movement of virtual currency holdings to traditional currencies and *vice versa*. Regulatory authorities in many jurisdictions are highly sensitive to the currency conversion function and require some form of approval and oversight for parties providing currency conversion services. In the United States, the State of New York recently granted its first authorization for a digital currency conversion service. The New York Department of Financial Services granted the bitcoin exchange, itBit, a public charter authorizing itBit to provide currency conversion services for bitcoin [39].

The potential utility of virtual currencies as a method to store economic value can make them useful additional tools for those nations in which the economy is unstable. In a sense, virtual currency used as an economic value storage mechanism parallels part of the appeal held by certain commodities, such as precious metals. In countries where the national currency is subject to rapid and extreme value fluctuations, commodities such as precious metals are often prized as value storage investments that provide a hedge against the economic instability. Virtual currencies can perform a similar role, with the added advantage that they are significantly more convenient to obtain, store, and manage than are most of the traditionally popular commodities.

Although virtual currencies are themselves subject to abrupt valuation shifts, they do have the potential to contribute to the economic stability of developing economies by providing an additional mechanism for collecting and retaining economic value. The increasingly global nature of the most popular digital currency platforms such as Bitcoin also helps to make the assets held by individuals to be more mobile, readily transferable to other countries. This mobility can be an important advantage for the owners of the assets, however, it can also be unsettling for national governments growing increasingly concerned that widespread use of digital currency can contribute to the rapid movement of economic assets out of their countries. To the extent that citizens in countries with unstable economies believe that digital currencies offer greater stability and mobility for their economic assets, they may prefer those electronic currencies to their established national currencies. By holding more of their assets in digital currency than in traditional currency, the citizens may actually undermine the traditional currency, making it less valuable and more volatile.

Consider, for example, the challenges facing Greece and its economy. The substantial uncertainty regarding that nation's future in the European Community has had devastating consequences for the people and businesses of the country. In that type of highly unsettled economic environment, digital currency options may begin to appear significantly more attractive to the people and enterprises than may be the case in thriving and stable economies. When a nation's economic conditions deteriorate to the point where there are dramatic shifts in currency value and availability, virtual currencies can provide a useful option for all parties. Although digital currencies are notorious for substantial value shifts, they may under some circumstance provide more effective opportunities for protecting asset value and ensuring access to those assets than the traditional national currency provides.

At present, no form of digital currency has been recognized as official fiat currency anywhere in the world. As noted previously, although efforts such as those underway in Ecuador have been characterized as national digital currency initiatives, those programs do not, in fact, constitute true national virtual currency platforms. For the present and for the foreseeable future, no nation is likely to establish a real digital currency platform as its sole fiat currency system. Accordingly, the established framework of policies, laws, and regulations governing the creation and use of currency is not directly applicable to any form of digital currency. Development, distribution, and use of Bitcoin and other virtual currencies are beyond the current reach of official currency rules and regulators.

Although no country has yet built a fiat currency on a form of virtual currency, there are national initiatives that seek to integrate digital currency more fully into national economic infrastructures. For instance, the Isle of Man is currently developing a crypto-currency blockchain which it will manage to support expansion of digital currency use. The Department of Economic Development of the Isle of Man will establish and maintain the blockchain using the "Credits" cyrpto-currency platform [40]. Under this plan, the government of the Isle of Man will be one of the many different groups around the world that provide computing resources that support crypto-currencies.

The Isle of Man initiative illustrates a government approach to virtual currencies which could serve as a useful model for other jurisdictions. The Isle of Man is not creating a new digital currency. Instead, it has chosen to participate in an existing crypto-currency platform. It is not, as is the case in Ecuador, merely extending the reach of an existing national currency into an electronic payment network. The Isle of Man is becoming an active participant in a privately developed crypto-currency platform, the Credit system [41]. In this way, the government of the Isle of Man is, in effect, joining a virtual currency community which emerged through collaboration among willing private parties.

By joining an existing virtual currency blockchain, the government of the Isle of Man would obtain full visibility into the operations of the currency platform, the same information access as is available to all other blockchain participants. Additionally, participation would enable the government to influence the operations of the currency platform through direct activity instead of being forced to rely only on external regulatory oversight.

Government participation in a virtual currency platform also raises interesting legal and public policy issues for consideration. For instance, if a government participates in the mining of a digital currency, does the entire blockhain operation become a form of government action. In the United States, for example, actions undertaken by the national government are subject to certain legal requirements and constraints imposed by legislation, regulation, and even the United States Constitution. Similar actions taken by private individuals or entities are not subject to those same requirements and constraints. If a government participates directly in the creation and distribution of digital currency which had previously been entirely private, it is possible that some of the legal requirements and constraints associated with government action may then be applicable to the digital currency system. It is, at present, unclear whether or not government participation in a private virtual currency platform would transform that platform into a government operation, thus leading to mandatory compliance with all of the obligations and constraints associated with government action.

A growing number of nations now recognize the potential value of the blockchain technology at the core of Bitcoin and other crypto-currency systems. These governments recognize that the blockchain platform can effectively support a growing set of activities and transactions in addition to virtual currencies. The blockchain technology enables secure distributed transparent transactions, and that capability can be useful for governments as well as businesses in the future. For this reason, the Canadian Senate recently recognized the potential value of the blockchain and other virtual currency platform technologies, and it recommended that the Canadian government refrain from overly intrusive regulation of virtual currency systems to encourage development of methods through which the Canadian government can make use of virtual currency platform technologies [42].

The strategy of governments joining privately established virtual communities such as those based on bitcoin and Credits may offer the most productive and effective approach to government oversight of digital currency development. Under this approach, instead of focusing on regulation of the virtual currency platforms, governments can influence their operation through direct participation. The government of the Isle of Man is joining the crypto-currency community by agreeing to use its computing resources to host a portion of the blockchain which supports the operations of the community. As a member of the virtual currency platform, the government of the Isle of Man can help to encourage expanded use of digital currency systems.

When governments actively participate in Bitcoin and other digital currency platforms, they become members of the digital currency communities. For example, in the Isle of Man situation, to the extent that government computers are joining the virtual currency network as active nodes, they can participate in the full range of community activities, including not only the use of the currency but also functions such as mining and transaction confirmation. In addition, as members of the virtual currency community, the government participants have full visibility into all network transactions and the full payment history.

As participants in digital currency blockchains, governments will have full access to the public ledger documenting the transaction history of those blockchains. In this setting, presumably there would be no need for court order or subpoenas to access transaction information, as the governments would have full access to all available transaction documentation as a result of their membership in the community and participation in the network. Viewed from this perspective, it seems that it would be in the best interest of governments to join all of the virtual currency networks as participants. By serving as active participants in those networks, the governments would obtain full access to network information and would have the ability to influence the activities of the networks. It is an open issue, however, as to the response of the digital currency communities if governments routinely agreed to join them. Some of those communities may be reluctant to be in a situation in which multiple governments are active members of their networks.

Some advocates of virtual currency recommend a form of government-backed digital currency that is even more expansive than that proposed by the government of the Isle of Man. They propose full integration of the networked computing and public ledger platforms used extensively in the digital currency environment to support use of a new form of digital currency backed by the national government [43]. This true national digital currency need not necessarily be linked to the country's existing fiat currency, but could instead be an entirely new currency. The key, however, would be full backing and support for the new currency by the national government. Only if the government guarantees the value of the new digital currency can it be viewed as a form of true national currency.

Increasingly, digital currency networks are connecting with other established systems for money transfer. For instance, electronic money transfer platforms are already extremely popular among people from developing countries who are working in other parts of the world and who regularly send payments back to their families in their home countries. Some of the most popular of these electronic money transfer services are provided through use of mobile phone networks. Bitcoin and other virtual currency systems are now integrating with these established mobile platforms for international money transfer. The M-Pesa mobile payment system is extremely popular in African nations including Kenya and Nigeria, where it processes millions of dollars worth of money transfers from Kenyans and Nigerians working in developed countries sent to their families at home, and that system is now integrated with Bitcoin, providing a digital currency capability for the processing of some of those international money transfers [44].

In most nations, the regulatory authority of national banks and the government agencies responsible for oversight of fiat currency is extremely limited. Most of those entities are merely responsible for the protection of the integrity of the national currency. They generally execute that responsibility by protecting the value of the national currency and by preserving citizen confidence in the value of the national currency. Accordingly, most currency regulators do not have legal jurisdiction simply to ban or prohibit use of virtual currencies. Instead, any actions those regulators take affecting digital currencies must be presented as activities necessary to protect the value of the national currency or to preserve citizen confidence in the national currency. To the extent that those authorities have jurisdiction over the conduct of banks and other financial institutions, that jurisdiction can also serve as the basis for regulatory action affecting virtual currencies.

As private payment platforms, virtual currency systems are not directly subject to oversight by national currency regulators. It is now common, however, for those regulators to take the position that use of digital currencies is now sufficiently widespread to merit warnings to the public as to potential risk, and regulatory action regarding the extent to which banks and other financial institutions can use digital currencies. Additionally, national currency regulators now commonly take the position that the conversion process between traditional currencies and virtual currencies affects the value of traditional currencies and the integrity of the national currency system, thus the regulators exercise oversight over the conversion process.

Traditional regulators of national currencies do not have sufficient legal authority to prevent all use of virtual currencies. They do, however, have sufficient authority to complicate and impede the development of those currencies and the expansion of digital currency applications. The exercise of that authority is conducted, not through direct controls over the digital currencies, but instead through oversight powers regarding financial institutions and the overall integrity of the national currency.

Matsuura Chapter 4:
Digital Currency, The Challenge of Money Laundering, and a New Framework for the Regulation of Currency

CHAPTER 4

Digital Currency, The Challenge of Money Laundering, and a New Framework for the Regulation of Currency

Abstract: Laws and regulations directed against money laundering are some of the most active legal compliance obligations facing the virtual currency community globally. Authorities fear use of digital currencies for money laundering and for direct financing of illegal conduct due in large part to the largely anonymous and international nature of virtual currency systems. In most jurisdictions, existing rules against money laundering have either been interpreted to address digital currencies or are being specifically modified to provide expressly such coverage. Anti-money laundering requirements are most frequently presented in the form of "know your customer" requirements, transaction monitoring obligations, and mandatory reporting rules. These requirements are most commonly applied to "money services businesses" which include banks and other financial institutions as well as money transmitters, money transfer services, and exchange trading and conversion service providers. Anti-money laundering laws and regulations present some of the most significant current legal compliance obligations facing the virtual currency community around the world.

Keywords: California, Connecticut, digital currency, dirty money, documentation, Financial Crimes Enforcement Network (FinCEN), Isle of Man, know your customer requirements, money laundering, money services businesses (MSBs), money transfer, money transmission, North Carolina, record-keeping, reporting requirements, Singapore, transaction monitoring, United States Treasury Department, Washington.

Money laundering is the process through which economic gain derived from illegal conduct is converted into apparently innocent forms of financial value. For example, money acquired through sale of illegal goods or services is frequently used to purchase legal products or invested into legal business operations. The illegally obtained cash is converted into legal products or activities, thus apparently "laundering" or cleaning the "dirty" funds. Concern by governments around the world as to the potential use of virtual currencies to facilitate money laundering and payments in support of illegal activities seems to be one of the most significant factors inciting those governments to review and monitor the development of digital currency systems.

Assume for example, that an organization operates an illegal gambling operation. All of the money it receives as a result of the illegal gambling activities it

Jeffrey H. Matsuura
All rights reserved-© 2016 Bentham Science Publishers

facilitates is considered to be dirty money, legally tainted by the fact that it was earned through illegal activities. If the organization then invests the dirty money into a business to purchase an ownership interest in the legitimate business, the organization will be entitled to a share of the earnings of that legitimate business. That ownership share of the legitimate business generates money that is clean and not legally tainted. Through this process, the organization engaged in the illegal gambling operations has exchanged its dirty money for clean funds, thus laundering its legally tainted earnings.

The money laundering process is illegal. It is unlawful to benefit from illegally acquired gains. It is also illegal for an individual or an enterprise to accept funds that it knows or should have reason to know were obtained from illegal conduct. It is thus illegal both to launder dirty money and to assist in the laundering process. Emphasis on controlling money laundering is largely based on the premise that if it is more difficult to convert illegal funds into clean funds, the process of identifying and penalizing illegal conduct can be more effective and efficient.

Money laundering is a major concern with regard to digital currencies. The global reach of digital currencies and the potential for essentially anonymous value exchanges using digital currencies make these digital value exchanges highly popular for individuals and enterprises engaged in illegal conduct. For this reason, a growing number of governments now insist that existing laws and regulation directed against money laundering should also be applied to digital currency transactions. Concern about the potential of digital currency to facilitate and encourage money laundering has been expressed by virtually every government that has considered issues associated with digital currency use [45]. This concern is so widespread that essentially every country and region attracted by the potential economic benefits of digital currency use is also seriously troubled by potential illegal use of the virtual currency platforms.

A growing number of jurisdictions now specifically apply existing laws and regulations directed against money laundering to digital currency. One of the most common first steps when a government begins to address the issue of digital currencies is the direct application of money laundering controls to virtual currency systems. For instance, the Isle of Man amended its law against money laundering to address specifically the activities of digital currency operations. Digital currency trading exchanges and other businesses that facilitate trade of virtual currencies are now specifically covered by the Isle of Man's Proceeds of Crime Act of 2008 [46]. It is also worth noting, that in most instances existing laws against money laundering can easily be enforced in the digital currency environment without any specific amendments or modifications to accomplish that purpose. Anti-money laundering rules are generally written broadly enough to address essentially all methods of value exchange. It seems however that governments frequently take special action clarifying that digital currencies are within the scope of laws against money laundering in order to make a political statement. Even absent such action, however, restrictions against money laundering are effective in the virtual currency environment in addition to the traditional monetary systems.

Regulations directed against money laundering generally focus on several key topics. They commonly place an obligation on parties involved with financial transactions to report instances of suspected money laundering and to cooperate with authorities to investigate and prevent laundering. Additionally, anti-laundering requirements commonly impose "know your customer" obligations. These obligations force parties involved in financial transactions to obtain basic information from all participants in the transactions. Parties that facilitate financial transactions are expected to know the true identity of the parties involved in the transactions and basic contact information. Anti-money laundering laws and regulations are, at their heart, recording-keeping and transaction monitoring requirements. They are not so much aimed at directly stopping money laundering as they are intended to make such laundering easier for authorities to identify and to force creation of documentation which can facilitate future legal action against the parties involved in the laundering.

Concern about money laundering has a direct and significant impact on regulatory oversight of digital currency. The potential for near anonymity with digital currency systems, and the global reach of those systems make them popular vehicles for laundering efforts. It is not difficult to transform illegally obtained money into digital currency and either use that currency for transactions or convert the digital currency back into traditional currency. Either process successfully assists the money launderer to clean the funds.

In addition to its potential role in money laundering, virtual currencies also raise concern among law enforcement authorities based on their popularity for use as the payment vehicle of choice in many illegal transactions. Parties selling illegal goods and services now frequently seek payment in Bitcoin or other virtual currency. In these instances the digital currency is used to pay for the illegal product or activity. These cases do not constitute money laundering, but they also erode the public reputation of digital currencies by linking those currencies with illegal conduct, in the perception of much of the public.

Emerging standard practice appears to involve direct application of existing anti-money laundering laws and regulations to digital currency transactions [47]. At present, it is fair to assert that regulatory oversight directed against money laundering provides the most convenient and most actively used conceptual legal framework to support regulatory oversight of digital currencies and the parties who use them. The same requirements involving transaction monitoring and reports to government authorities are now commonly applied to both traditional and digital currency transactions. To accomplish this task, the various parties involved in the digital currency business chain, including those who transmit and store digital currency, as well as those who perform conversion between traditional currency and digital currency, are now routinely required to comply with all anti-money laundering obligations.

Governments around the world now routinely make use of their anti-money laundering controls as the vehicle of choice to enforce regulatory oversight as to virtual currency operations. Controls against money laundering are most frequently applied through regulation of money transmission activities, thus those rules now appear to be the leading and most widely applied legal compliance requirements affecting the virtual currency community around the world. Provisions directed against money laundering are most actively enforced against the financial institutions and other parties that process money transfers and money transmission. To the extent that virtual currencies provide an effective and popular vehicle for the transfer of economic value, they are now widely viewed to fall within the scope of the rules designed to limit money laundering.

Concerned about the potential use of digital currencies for money laundering, the government of Singapore adjusted its financial regulatory framework to include specifically digital currencies within the scope of its laws prohibiting money laundering [48]. Singapore granted the governmental agency, the Monetary Authority of Singapore (MAS) the responsibility for preventing use of digital currencies for money laundering. All parties who buy, sell or facilitate exchange of digital currencies in Singapore are required to verify the identity of their customers and to report all suspicious transactions to the MAS. These requirements for digital currencies parallel those imposed for traditional transactions.

The regulatory approach adopted in Singapore illustrates that money laundering regulations applied to digital currency frequently include prohibitions against use of those digital assets in support of terrorist organizations and activities. Most jurisdictions that enforce anti-money laundering rules also use those rules to combat terrorism. In Singapore, it is illegal to use digital currencies to provide financial assistance to terrorists and terrorist organizations. Prohibitions against financial aid for terrorist activities are commonly incorporated into anti-money laundering laws.

Another aspect of the battle against money laundering in the context of virtual currencies involves oversight of parties who transfer money. Frequently referred to as money transmitters, these organizations enable people to send money to others. An important component of the regulations applied to money transmitters is an effort to prevent use of money transmitters to facilitate money laundering. Increasingly, laws and rules applied to money transmitters specifically address digital currency services and systems. It is now common for jurisdictions to consider virtual currency platforms to be money transmitters.

Authorities in California, for example, are considering how to integrate virtual currency systems into the rules governing money transmitters. The California Department of Business Oversight regulates financial institutions, including money transmitters, operating in California. The Department is presently evaluating whether to assert its existing rules for money transmitters to digital currency systems through its own regulations or to request specific legislative action on the subject from the California legislature [49].

The North Carolina legislature is also addressing the issue of virtual currencies as money transmission systems. The North Carolina House of Representatives approved legislation which would specifically include virtual currencies systems as money transmitters for regulatory purposes through its North Carolina Money Transmittal Act (House Bill 289) [50]. This legislation, if fully enacted, would amend the laws establishing regulatory oversight of money transmitters to specify that digital currency platforms are money transmitters.

Legislation under consideration in Connecticut also specifically includes virtual currencies within the scope of money transmission services [51]. The Connecticut Banking Department is the government agency in that state tasked with the responsibility for oversight of money transmission activities. The pending legislation in Connecticut would require that all applicants for Connecticut money transmission licenses disclose if they intend to offer any digital currency services. Based upon such disclosures, the Banking Department would be authorized to accept, reject or accept with additional conditions the applications for money transmission authority involving digital currency [52].

Authorities in the state of Washington have also concluded that virtual currency transfer constitutes a form of money transmission for regulatory purposes. In Washington, money transmissions are regulated by the Department of Financial Institutions. State authorities in Washington now include Bitcoin and other digital currencies as part of the money transmission process. Accordingly, the Department of Financial Institutions now has jurisdiction over digital currency use in Washington as part of its authority over money transmission activities in that state [53].

At the federal level in the United States, the Treasury Department plays a leading role in efforts to prevent money laundering. The key component of the Treasury's effort is the Financial Crimes Enforcement Network (FinCEN) [54]. The FinCEN system attempts to restrict money laundering by regulating money services businesses (MSBs) under the terms of the Bank Secrecy Act and associated legislation. FinCEN operates a framework of registration, monitoring, and reporting requirements directed toward MSBs. These regulatory activities comprise a significant component of the money laundering control process in the United States.

An important focus of FinCEN actions at present is the virtual currency working environment. FinCEN continues to refine the scope of its oversight of digital currency operations. To the extent that participants in the digital currency ecosystem are characterized by FinCEN as MSBs, they are subject to regulatory oversight as part of the Treasury Department's anti-money laundering program. Currently, individuals and businesses that make use of virtual currencies for the sale and purchase of goods and services are not deemed to be MSBs and are accordingly not subject to FinCEN regulatory oversight [55]. Similarly, parties who mine, create, Bitcoin and other virtual currencies for their own use are not regulated by FinCEN [56]. Businesses and other organizations that purchase or sell digital currency for their own benefit are not regulated by FinCEN, and parties who develop software that enables or supports digital currency creation, distribution or use are not within the scope of FinCEN oversight [57].

FinCEN regulation does, however, extend into certain aspects of the virtual currency environment. For example, digital currency exchanges and the parties who administer those exchanges are within the scope of FinCEN regulatory oversight [58]. This means that those parties and institutions must register with

FinCEN, and must comply with the transaction monitoring and reporting requirements applied by FinCEN to MSBs [59]. FinCEN controls are also applicable to parties providing conversion services that process exchanges between virtual currencies and formal national currencies. The FinCEN approach to regulation generally attempts to restrict oversight to those parties in the digital currency ecosystem who are providing services on a commercial basis, not those who are merely using those currencies for their own business or personal purchases and sales.

Under the current U.S. national framework for money laundering controls, the critical distinction for regulatory purposes is the identification of those portions of the virtual currency marketplace that are deemed to be MSBs. At present, individual and business users of digital currencies are not defined to be MSBs to the extent that their use of digital currencies is for their own beneficial purposes, either in the course of transactions or investments. The developers and distributors of software that enables and supports the creation, distribution, and use of digital currencies, and the parties who create (mine) those currencies are also outside of the scope of MSB regulation. However, the parties and organizations that facilitate the trading of virtual currencies or the conversion of those currencies to traditional currency forms are viewed as MSBs and are subject to U.S. federal laws directed against money laundering.

Advocates of Bitcoin and other digital currencies appear to be divided as to the efforts by different jurisdictions to focus attention on application of rules against money laundering to virtual currency systems. Some believe that those government actions may impede the growth and diversification of digital currency use. Others contend that it is entirely appropriate to include digital currency systems within the oversight of anti-money laundering rules, and that such regulation may enhance the popularity of virtual currencies by providing users with greater confidence as to the safety and integrity of those systems.

Perhaps the most accurate characterization of the situation is that application of rules against money laundering to virtual currency networks is inevitable. To the extent that those networks are used to transfer economic value, it seems clear that they should be placed within the scope of the rules designed to prohibit money laundering. It seems that, when digital currency systems operate as value exchange platforms, the rules against money laundering should be applicable even if those rules do not specifically identify virtual currency systems as money transmitters. It should also be recognized, however, that virtual currency platforms increasingly support activities and applications that may not involve exchange of economic value. When digital currency platforms are used for those other applications, they may not be operating as money transmitters, thus there seems to be little justification for application of the anti-money laundering requirements in that context. As the uses of virtual currency networks diversify, it will be increasingly important to ensure that regulatory oversight applied to those networks remains consistent with the actual activities of each network. When a digital currency system functions as a medium for exchange of economic value, application of rules against money laundering is appropriate. When a virtual currency platform supports other activities, such oversight would not be appropriate.

The framework for application of record-keeping, monitoring, and reporting requirements associated with anti-money laundering regulations emerging through the United States Treasury's FinCEN system seems to provide a useful model for other jurisdictions. The FinCEN approach applies anti-money laundering requirements only to certain functions in the virtual currency marketplace. It does not apply those requirements to individual and business users of the currencies or to the parties who develop the software and other technologies that support and sustain the digital currency platforms. Instead, it applies the rules to those parties engaged in the business of operating the trading exchanges where virtual currencies are bought, sold, and converted to traditional currencies.

The FinCEN approach appears to strike a reasonable balance between the need for effective regulatory oversight to reduce the scope of money laundering while also avoiding unnecessary impediments to the development and growth of digital currency applications. This system provides an effective basis for identifying and blocking money laundering while reducing the compliance burdens placed on the virtual currency community.

CHAPTER 5

Digital Currency as a Commodity

Abstract: In many jurisdictions, virtual currencies are, at least in some contexts, viewed to be a commodity, a form of property. Classification of digital currency as property has substantial and far-reaching legal consequences. Digital currencies are now traded through trading exchanges. Future contracts and other forms of financial derivatives based upon virtual currencies are also bought and sold in marketplaces. Enterprises such as LedgerX and TerraExchange are now seeking full regulatory approval to permit them to function as authorized trading exchanges able to serve as trading markets for a wide range of financial products. Recognition of digital currencies as property has profound tax consequences. It makes digital currency potentially subject to the laws of debtor/creditor relations when the currency is held as an asset. Digital currency as property is subject to diverse laws including laws of wills, estates, and trusts, when the currency is part of an individual's personal estate. Laws and international treaties governing foreign investment in assets are in some cases applicable to trans-border purchase of virtual currency. Digital currency is already widely viewed to be a form of property in many jurisdictions, and in that capacity, it is currently potentially subject to a substantial and diverse set of rules addressing property ownership and transfer.

Keywords: Asset, commodities, Commodities Future Trading Exchange (CFTC), creditor, derivatives, financial instruments, foreign investment, future, intangible, LedgerX, lien, Mt. Gox, OKCoin, property, tax, TeraExchange, trade agreements, trading exchange, wills.

Articles of commerce that are bought and sold are frequently characterized as commodities. A very wide range of goods are regularly traded and thus recognized as commodities. When considering commercial commodities, we often think of goods such as agricultural products and precious metals. The universe of traded commodities is however, far more extensive than the handful of goods that most rapidly come to mind. It is becoming increasingly apparent that individuals and organizations in different parts of the world now consider Bitcoin and other forms of digital currency to be property which can be effectively used in commerce as a commodity.

Commodities can also include intangible goods. Just as gold or wheat can be commercially traded and thus qualify as commodities, so too can intangible products be the subject of commercial trading as commodities. Digital currency as represented by the "tokens" that identify it can be recognized as intangible goods. Accordingly, digital currency and other electronic goods can serve as commodities.

Jeffrey H. Matsuura
All rights reserved-© 2016 Bentham Science Publishers

When viewed as a commodity, digital currency can be linked to financial derivatives, the range of financial instruments that facilitate trading of the financial risks associated with the fluctuating value of a commodity. Derivatives are financial instruments that are based upon specific commodities or other financial instruments or indicators [60]. Derivatives reflect financial risks associated with a specific commodity and they are traded on financial exchanges. By selling and buying derivatives, parties can obtain and transfer financial risks, thus enabling them to manage their exposure to future financial risks through processes including hedging, arbitrage, and speculation.

In the context of commodities, derivatives include contracts providing for future purchase or sale of specific commodities at specific prices. These future contracts or future are financial instruments that derive their value from the shifting prices of the commodities to which they are linked. If a party owns a contract for the future purchase of a commodity and the market price of that commodity rises above the future contract price, the party derives economic benefit from the fact that it could actually purchase the commodity at a below market price and also from the fact that it could sell the contract at a premium price to another party who seeks to purchase the commodity at the favorable price. In contrast, if a party owns a future contract which establishes a future price that proves to be higher then the future market price, the owner of that contract is in an unfavorable position.

Trading of financial derivatives, including future contracts, is regulated by government authorities. In the United States, for example, the lead regulator for commodity future is the Commodity Futures Trading Commission (CFTC). The primary mission of regulatory agencies such as the CFTC is to preserve the integrity of commodity trading, including oversight of both the trades and the markets in which the trades are processed.

Digital currency, as a commodity, can serve as the basis for future contracts and other forms of financial derivative. Parties can for instance, enter into future contracts based on future prices for bitcoins and other forms of virtual currency. As is the case with traditional commodities such as oil and agricultural products, consenting parties can enter into binding agreements for the purchase and sale of digital currency at a specific price as of a specific future date. In the case of future contracts, the key financial transactions are the purchase and sale of contracts, not the actual commodity itself. Future contracts for digital currency can be applied for risk management in the same manner as those contracts have long been used in the context of traditional commodities. Future contracts and other financial derivatives have already been executed and traded through digital currency trading exchanges such as, OK Coin [61]. Regulatory authorities such as the CFTC are aware of these emerging derivatives exchanges for digital currency, and they now assert oversight jurisdiction over those markets and the trades they process [62].

At present, the CFTC is considering the first formal application from a virtual currency trading exchange [63]. LedgerX has formally applied for authority from the CFTC to operate an exchange and clearinghouse for derivatives involving Bitcoin [64]. Although other exchanges are reportedly currently already processing virtual currency future trades, LedgerX is apparently the first such exchange to seek full formal regulatory authority in the United States to serve as an exchange and clearinghouse for those transactions. If LedgerX receives CFTC authorization, it will operate as the first fully regulated digital currency derivates trading exchange. In that capacity, LedgerX will be subject to the full range of CFTC oversight and controls, providing a future trading environment for virtual currencies that matches traditional regulated exchanges.

Derivative agreements based on Bitcoin are also traded on the TeraExchange [65]. The TeraExchange provides a market for swapping Bitcoin contracts [66]. TeraExchange, like LedgerX, has requested CFTC approval for its operations [67]. When CFTC approval is obtained, TeraExchange will apparently function as a fully regulated derivatives market devoted to future agreements involving Bitcoin and presumably other virtual currencies as time progresses. By pursuing full CFTC regulatory authority to operate as financial derivative exchanges processing Bitcoin-based future agreements, both LedgerX and TeraExchange represent a formalization of virtual currency derivatives. When these trading markets receive full regulatory approval, they will provide important additions to the derivatives trading environment.

Commodities are, from a legal perspective, forms of property that can be sold, bought, and otherwise processed. A growing number of authorities now recognize digital currency as a form of property. Although intangible in nature, some jurisdictions identify digital currency as property which is subject to the full range of legal requirements and protections afforded to property. When considered to be property, digital currency is characterized as personal property, in contrast to the class of property applied to land known as real property. When classified as property, virtual currencies are subject to a comprehensive and well-established framework of laws applicable to the diverse range of traditional goods.

The Isle of Man is one of several jurisdictions around the world presently in the process of revising its legal and regulatory environment in an effort to facilitate expanded use of digital currency and to attract businesses involved in the digital currency system. As part of that overall effort, the Isle of Man specifically determined that digital currency was not currency but was instead a form of property, subject to existing rights and obligations associated with personal property [68]. It is noteworthy that this jurisdiction eager to encourage more extensive digital currency use opted to clarify that digital currency is, in fact, a form of personal property.

Spanish authorities also appear to take the position that digital currencies are not money but are instead digital goods. As digital goods, it seems that Bitcoin and other virtual currencies in use in Spain are governed by rules associated with barter included in the Civil Code of Spain [69]. In this context, transactions involving digital currencies in Spain are viewed as barter trades, and the existing civil laws governing such trades are applicable.

Characterization of digital currency as personal property carries numerous legal implications. For instance, if digital currency is personal property, then presumably it is subject to personal property taxes. In much the same way that the estimated value of automobiles is taxed in some jurisdictions, so too presumably would holdings of digital currency be subject to personal property tax assessments. It seems likely that some jurisdictions will require individuals to report the commercial value of their digital currency holding. The jurisdictions that treat digital currency as personal property would then presumably assess tax on that property subject to the existing personal property tax rate. The economic value of digital currency holdings is, at present, highly volatile, subject to notable rises and falls over time. That fluctuation in value may require regular re-assessment of value for property tax purposes in a manner similar to the process used to adjust tax value of real estate in many jurisdictions.

In jurisdictions in which some sort of tax is assessed in conjunction with sales of goods, it is possible that tax and revenue authorities might view the sale of digital currency as a taxable transaction. Sales tax and value added tax, for example, could be assessed in some jurisdictions in association with sale and purchase of digital currency. In this environment, sale of digital currency could trigger a requirement to collect sales or value-added tax based on the value of the digital currency sold.

The Australian Tax Office indicated that purchases in Australia using digital currency are subject to Australian Goods and Services Tax [70]. Australian goods and services sales that make use of digital currencies for payment are viewed as commercial transactions that are subject to traditional Australian sales tax obligations. This approach seems appropriate, as purchases made using digital currencies for payment do not differ in any material way from sales involving traditional payment forms. Other national authorities, such as the government of Singapore have also indicated they would apply goods and services taxes, at lest under some circumstances, for purchases made using virtual currency. However, concern has been expressed that Australian authorities may also assess the Goods and Services Tax for the purchase of virtual currency. If purchase of digital currency is taxed as a sale, then digital currency owners will, in effect be taxed twice, once when they buy their virtual currency and a second time when they use that currency to purchase other products.

State sales tax authorities in the state of New York expressly stated that New York state sales tax is not applicable to the sale of virtual currency [71]. The New York authorities concluded that digital currencies are intangible property and are thus not subject to sales tax when they are purchased. New York authorities also indicate, however, that the purchase of certain goods and services using virtual currency for payment would require collection of sales tax and associated sales reporting.

The decision by New York tax authorities to characterize virtual currency as intangible property not subject to traditional sales tax seems to be a reasonable approach, however, it can also carry interesting potential tax issues. For instance, instead of applying traditional sales tax to intangible property, some jurisdictions now apply specialized taxes when that intangible property (computer software, for example) is sold. Additionally, in some jurisdictions, taxes are assessed based on rights of use for property (use taxes) instead of for the purchase of the property. In jurisdictions such as New York where virtual currency is expressly characterized as intangible property for tax purposes, it is essential to examine the extent, if any, to which intangible property is subject to other taxes associated with its distribution or use. Exemption from traditional sales tax does not automatically mean that there are no tax implications associated with sale or use of virtual currency.

It is useful to consider the ways in which jurisdictions have approached intangible products such as computer software when anticipating their likely application of sales tax to virtual currency. In the United States, the Internal Revenue Service (IRS) considers intellectual property rights associated with goods such as computer software to be "intangibles." For the IRS and other tax authorities, intangible assets are generally viewed to be assets that are non-monetary and lacking any tangible physical manifestation. These intangible assets are viewed by the IRS as capital assets and the costs associated with their acquisition can be amortized over a period of fifteen years [72]. It currently remains unclear as to whether or not the IRS would consider virtual currency to be an intangible capital asset subject to its existing rules on intangibles, however, it appears that reasonable arguments can be made in favor of such a characterization.

Jurisdictions generally assess income taxes against earning that are generated by intangible assets, just as they do for income from tangible assets [73]. Accordingly, it is reasonable to assume that income earned from the sale of bitcoin and other virtual currencies is subject to income taxes. The issue of whether or not such income is treated as ordinary income or some form of capital gain will vary from jurisdiction to jurisdiction and is not yet resolved. In large part, that tax determination will likely depend on the extent to which virtual currency is viewed as a capital asset, personal property or some type of financial service.

Some jurisdictions apply a lower income tax rate to income generated by intangible assets. This benefit is often applied by jurisdictions attempting to attract businesses that create and use intangible assets, such as intellectual property. To the extent that virtual currency is characterized as an intangible asset, it is possible that the reduced income tax rates offered by some jurisdictions to attract industries based on intangible assets could be applicable to virtual currency services such as trading, conversion, and storage. It is thus likely that businesses operating in the virtual currency ecosystem may have incentive to locate in those jurisdictions around the world which provide favorable income tax treatment to earnings generated by intangible assets.

If deemed to be personal property, digital currency would presumably also be subject to legal provisions associated with the transfer of property upon death of the owner. In this context, digital currency could be transferred to heirs through wills, with such transfers presumably subject to estate taxes. Individuals engaged in estate planning should now include their digital currency holdings as part of their assets as they create their wills, trusts, and other legal documents. In order to accomplish this transfer effectively, individuals who own bitcoins and other digital currencies must ensure that all account and other information necessary to access and transfer the virtual currency holdings is made available to executors and trustees involved with the estate. Additionally, providers of wallet and other digital currency account services must now be prepared to process digital currency holdings as part of probate and trust management processes. The parties who manage personal digital currency accounts must adopt and implement policies, practices, and procedures for effectively handling account transfer and liquidation requests that are made as a result of the probate of wills and the management of trusts. The value of digital currency transferred in an estate would likely be included in the calculation of the value of the estate in order to determine estate tax obligations.

In the United States, the majority of states apply state sales tax to at least some transactions involving computer software. The states of Hawaii, New Mexico, South Dakota, Tennessee, and Texas apply sales tax to all computer software sales [74]. Prudence suggests that parties engaged in virtual currency sales in jurisdictions in which purchases of software through downloads are taxed should obtain legal advice regarding the extent to which sales tax may be applicable to the sale of digital currency.

A variety of jurisdictions also apply use taxes based on the value of goods that are used by parties in these jurisdictions. These taxes are not assessed for the sale of the goods, but are instead applied based on their use. Use taxes are most commonly applied to tangible goods, however, it is nonetheless prudent to review their applicability and scope when a party is collecting or storing virtual currency. Even if sales taxes are not applicable for the purchase of digital currency in a jurisdiction, it is possible that use tax may come into play to the extent that the digital currency acquired is to be collected or stored.

Some jurisdictions are beginning to apply taxes similar to use taxes in the context of leased computing capacity. For instance Chicago, Illinois in the United States now applies a tax to certain cloud computing content and activities [75]. One portion of that tax is directed toward leased computer capacity applied toward certain functions. Although storage and other processing of virtual currency are apparently not specifically identified as forms of leased computing use within the scope of the Chicago tax, they do not seem to be specifically excluded from the tax. Accordingly, it remains possible that the Chicago tax could at some point be interpreted to apply digital currency creation, sharing, and processing functions conducted through use of leased or shared computing facilities. Similarly, those key virtual currency activities could also fall within the scope of similar taxes directed toward leased computing use which may be implemented by other jurisdictions in the future.

Jurisdictions that apply value-added tax (VAT) to sales are currently considering the extent to which VAT should be applied to sale of virtual currency. The European Court of Justice (ECJ) is currently considering that issue in a case it received from Sweden [76]. Swedish courts ruled that VAT is not applicable to sale of digital currency, however, the Swedish tax authority requested that the ECJ review that decision [77]. Currently in Europe, authorities in the United Kingdom, Germany, France, Belgium, Finland, and Spain have determined that VAT should not be applied to sale of virtual currencies, however, authorities in Estonia and Poland contend that VAT should be applied to those sales [78].

The government of Switzerland has reportedly taken the position that bitcoin and other digital currencies are not subject to VAT [79]. The Swiss Federal Tax Administration views transfer of virtual currency to be a financial activity but not delivery of any goods or services. Accordingly, VAT should not be assessed to these virtual currency transfers. Instead, the Swiss tax authority views Bitcoin and other digital currency transactions to be forms of financial intermediation which must comply with anti-money laundering and other requirements imposed by Swiss banking laws.

The Norwegian Tax Authority takes the position that VAT is applicable to certain sales of Bitcoin and other digital currencies. When a commercial party sells a virtual currency, that transaction is, according to the Norwegian Tax Authority, an electronic service, and such services are subject to the 25 percent VAT applied by Norwegian law [80]. Thus in Norway, commercial parties selling digital currencies are engaged in a commercial electronic service which is subject to VAT.

As personal property, it seems likely that digital currency could be included in property held in trust for the benefit of a party. Digital currency could also presumably be given to other parties in the form of a charitable donation or a traditional gift. When distributed as a gift, the value of the digital currency given would likely be subject to any applicable gift taxes. When donated to a qualified charity, the value of the digital currency at the time of donation could be eligible for use as a deduction to reduce

If categorized as property, virtual currencies can be treated as collateral in support of loans. Lenders commonly obtain a security interest in the property of the parties who receive the loans. A security interest associated with a loan provides a legally enforceable interest for the lender. If the borrower fails to meet the terms of the loan, the lender can use the property of the borrower to satisfy the debt obligations. In many instances, that security interest applies to essentially all of the property owned by the borrower. Thus if a borrower defaults on a loan, a creditor may be able to satisfy the obligation owed to it by seizing virtually any of the property owned by the borrower.

Some observers argue that if digital currency is property, it would be subject to seizure by creditors who have security interests in the property of the currency owner. For example, under the principles established by Article 9 of the Uniform Commercial Code (UCC), a framework for the law of contracts and commercial transactions which has been adopted in all of states in the United States, virtual currencies would be subject to blanket liens if they are deemed to be property [81]. It should also be noted that the security interest held by the lender under the principles of the UCC is associated with the property even after that property has been sold or otherwise transferred to another party. Thus under the UCC framework, if a buyer purchased an automobile, paying for the car with bitcoin and a third party held a security interest in the buyer's property as collateral for a loan, the third party would, under UCC principles, have the right to seize the bitcoin to satisfy debt owed, despite the fact that the bitcoin was no longer the property of the buyer.

If virtual currency is categorized as property, then all encumbrances associated with virtual currency follow that currency from owner to owner. This would make transactions involving digital currencies more complicated than those involving cash. If digital currency is property, than commercial transactions involving digital currency are, in effect, barter transactions involving exchange of property. Creditors may have claims vested in the digital currency which will remain enforceable against all future owners of the currency. In this environment, we can expect parties who accept virtual currency as payment to establish enforceable contractual arrangements with the buyers who use the virtual currency for payment. For example, before accepting digital currency as payment for a purchase, the seller might require the buyer to enter into a contract in which the buyer represents that there are no current or potential liens encumbering the digital currency and promises to indemnify the seller for all payments and costs the seller incurs in the event that a creditor of the buyer enforces a lien against the digital currency conveyed in the transaction.

In the United States, the Internal Revenue Service (IRS) seems to be supporting the characterization of virtual currency s property. The IRS specifically recognized digital currency as property [82]. Accordingly, for the IRS all transactions involving virtual currency are property transactions. As property transactions, they are governed by the same U.S. tax rules as are applied for traditional property transactions.

Increasingly, Bitcoin and other virtual currencies are effectively treated as forms of property. A growing number of jurisdictions are moving to officially recognize digital currency as property, however, even without such official action, governments, businesses, and individuals around the world now treat virtual currencies as property through their willingness to buy and sell the currencies in a manner consistent with traditional forms of property. Even without official government action designating virtual currencies as property, the behavior of participants in the global economy demonstrates that the market views digital currencies to be a form of property that has significant economic value.

Governments are now recognizing virtual currency as property through their actions, even without establishing formal definitions. For instance, the United States Department of Justice now routinely seizes digital currency among the other assets of defendants when the prosecutions involved include forfeiture of assets. Just as the U.S. law enforcement authorities seize automobiles and other personal property as part of the forfeiture process, so too are virtual currency holdings seized. U.S. authorities now seize bitcoin and other digital currency assets and then auction those assets as a mechanism to provide additional funds for use by the government [83]. For example, U.S. authorities recently auctioned more than 29,000 bitcoin seized as part of a criminal law prosecution associated with its "Silk Road" investigation [84]. As some observers noted, that auction was conducted with no constraints placed on future use of the bitcoin sold, thus apparently establishing the precedent that the U.S. government viewed the digital currency accumulated by the defendants to be fully fungible, not tainted by their alleged criminal conduct, and subject to no restrictions or limitations on their future use [85].

As virtual currency is now treated as property for purposes of forfeiture proceedings in criminal law cases, it will also likely be included in transactions associated with bankruptcy proceedings. As noted previously, digital currency is increasingly viewed among the assets treated as collateral for loans. In this role, bitcoins and other digital currencies will likely be used routinely to satisfy obligations held by creditors. The trustees and other parties responsible for managing the assets of a debtor in bankruptcy actions will be called upon to include virtual currency holdings among the debtor assets.

A high profile bankruptcy action in the world of virtual currency was centered on the Bitcoin trading exchange Mt. Gox. As a result of large-scale bitcoin theft, the Mt. Gox exchange ceased operations and entered bankruptcy [86]. As part of the bankruptcy process for Mt. Gox, the creditors involved designated another bitcoin exchange, Kraken, to assist Mt. Gox customers to place and resolve their claims against Mt. Gox [87].

Recognition of virtual currencies as a form of property can also result in application of international investment laws to those currencies. For example, virtually every nation in the world is a party to a set of international treaties widely known as Bilateral Investment Treaties (BITs). These treaties protect economic investments made by citizens of one nation in assets within the jurisdiction of another nation [88]. Thus for example if a Canadian company purchases ownership of a Turkish company or buys some other commercial asset in Japan, that investment is protected in part by the terms of the BIT which was executed by Canada and Turkey.

BITs provide basic protection for foreign investments in general [89]. For example, they require fair and equitable treatment for investments in a country that are held by citizens of the partner country. They also require that the investments owned by the foreign party be provided with full protection and security. BITs grant foreign parties the right to enforce their claims in a variety of international arbitration and dispute resolution forums.

If digital currencies are characterized as property, then it seems that purchase of those currencies should constitute an investment in the ownership or control of an asset of the sort addressed by BITs. Viewed from this perspective, for example, a citizen of the United Kingdom purchasing and holding bitcoin in Japan could claim protection for that investment under applicable terms of the BIT entered into by the United Kingdom and Japan. Under that protection, if the Japanese government or any of its agents took unfair actions adversely affecting the digital currency investment or if they failed to provide effective security or protection for the investment, then the U.K. owner of the bitcoin investment could apparently raise a claim against the Japanese government for violation of the BIT.

Parties considering substantial digital currency investments should review the framework of applicable investment laws prior to completing those investments and should familiarize themselves with the standard scope and terms of BITs [90]. It may be possible to structure those virtual currency holdings in a manner that provides greater legal protection for those investments. For instance, to the extent that digital currency holdings fall within the scope of BIT protection, it may be helpful to structure those holding to be within the jurisdiction of favorable BITs. Some nations, the Netherlands for example, are parties to many BITs with a wide range of other countries. For major virtual currency investments, it may be helpful to try to make sure that the party purchasing and holding ownership interest in the currency and the party providing the digital currency wallet storage support for the currency are located in countries connected to each other through a comprehensive BIT. This structure could provide the currency owner with the option of initiating an international arbitration action under the applicable BIT in the event that the country in which the digital currency holdings are located implements a regulatory or other action which undermines the economic value of the digital currency asset.

A variety of other international treaties may provide protections for foreign investments which could be applicable for virtual currency holding. For example, bilateral trade agreements and regional trade agreements such as the Trans-Pacific Partnership often address commitments made by the signatory nations to facilitate and protect investments made by citizens of one signatory in the jurisdiction of another signatory. The wide range of treaty terms and commitments that protect foreign investments can be useful in the context of digital currency ownership. Although these provisions may not prevent governments from banning, expropriating or otherwise limiting virtual currency holdings within their countries, these protections for foreign investments may provide digital currency owners with vehicles for seeking compensation or other recourse in the event that governments act to block or limit digital currency use.

If virtual currencies are to be characterized as property, for legal purposes, then international treaty and regulatory terms applicable to purchase, sale, and ownership of assets by foreign parties will likely be applicable to certain transactions involving those currencies. As noted previously, if digital currency is property, then purchase of that asset in another country and storage of that asset in the foreign country seems to constitute a foreign investment, subject to all the legal rights and obligations already applicable to such investments. When those asset holdings are transferred from the host country to another country, it is likely that at least some jurisdictions would view that transfer to constitute either international export of property or some form of repatriation of an asset. In either case, a well-established set of legal terms associated with the international movement of goods and assets would apply.

Review of the rapidly evolving legal landscape associated with virtual currencies suggests that those currencies will be characterized as different types of property and financial instruments depending upon the specific circumstances of any particular use. Accordingly, there seems to be no single answer to the questions as to whether digital currencies are conventional property, capital assets or a form of financial service. Depending on their actual use, it seems increasingly apparent that virtual currencies can qualify as any one of those diverse property or service forms. Virtual currency can be used in different ways and those different applications can result in characterization of the currency as different forms of property or as a type of financial service. Governments are increasingly aware of this chameleon-like capability associated with virtual currencies. Accordingly, authorities around the world now seem fully willing to apply multiple legal and regulatory schemes to digital currencies, depending on the specific details associated with each instance of actual use.

Matsuura Chapter 6:
Impact of Digital Currency on Commodity Trading and Markets

CHAPTER 6

Impact of Digital Currency on Commodity Trading and Markets

Abstract: Digital currency platforms are now in use to process trades involving virtual currencies and other financial products. Enterprises such as LedgerX and TeraExchange are now seeking full regulatory approval to use the cryptographically-based distributed computer networks pioneered by digital currency systems for use to support financial trading exchanges and markets. These systems will be subject to full regulatory oversight, as our existing traditional financial markets. The key capabilities of the digital currency platforms include security, transaction history transparency, and cost efficiency. Those characteristics can make valuable contributions to the future success of financial markets.

Keywords: CFTC, exchanges, ICBIT, LedgerX, markets, TeraExchange

To be an effective commodity, digital currency must be accessible for purchase and sale. This requires existence of markets where digital currency sellers and buyers can meet and transact business. Markets for digital currency trading are currently in active operation. The terms associated with those operations are evolving. The development and operation of virtual currency trading exchanges are subject to the existing legal requirements imposed by governments on financial markets.

The concept of regulation of trades involving digital currency as a commodity raises interesting and important issues and challenges. For example, an important characteristic of crypto-currency forms of digital currency, such as bitcoin, is their security and transparency. The technical process through which the crypto-currencies are created and transferred involves creation of a continuing and comprehensive record of transactions and interactions associated with the currencies. That record provides documentation of the integrity of the transactions, and it is accessible to all participants in the system. At least conceptually, the crypto-currency platforms enable individual users of those platforms to verify the integrity of the transactions and interactions processed by the platforms.

This environment enables individual users to review and consider the security and integrity of the transaction platform they are using. Theoretically, this capability reduces the need for oversight by an external party, such as a governmental

Jeffrey H. Matsuura
All rights reserved-© 2016 Bentham Science Publishers

regulator. When operating properly, crypto-currency platforms provide each user with visibility into the transaction history of the system sufficient to empower the user to make wise decisions regarding participation and transactions. Such visibility has traditionally been an important element of regulatory oversight associated with commodities transactions and all other financial interaction. To the extent that crypto-currency systems ensure transparency for users, they may require traditional regulators to alter their oversight role.

Markets have also merged to process trading of financial derivatives such as future contracts. As noted previously, commodity trading regulators such as the Commodities Futures Trading Commission in the United States have indicated they intend to assert jurisdiction over the operations of those exchanges, just as they oversee trading of derivatives associated with traditional commodities. Although informal markets for trading such as Predictious and ICBIT are now in operation, those markets have not yet requested formal regulatory authority to operate as full commodity future exchanges, and regulators including the CFTC have not yet required those exchanges to obtain regulatory approval [91]. For the present commodity trading regulators seem to be more interested in the activities of the traditional exchanges, intent upon requiring regulatory approval before those exchanges begin to process virtual currency contracts.

The LedgerX application for approval to operate as an exchange for derivatives trading has the potential to alter dramatically the role of virtual currency platforms in the commodities marketplace. If its application is approved, LedgerX would be the first fully regulated derivatives trading exchange operating through use of a distributed cryptographically-based computer network platform. LedgerX is prepared to submit to full CFTC regulation, and once operational as a fully authorized derivatives exchange, LedgerX will demonstrate that virtual currency platforms can be structured to support traditional financial marketplace functions consistent with the range of existing regulatory requirements associated with such markets. In effect, LedgerX will provide a proof of concept for use of secure distributed computer networks to operate financial trading exchanges. This verification is likely to have significant future consequences, paving the way for greater reliance on distributed computing networks to support financial trading markets that are more transparent and efficient than traditional exchanges.

Along with the LedgerX initiative, the application TeraExchange for approval for its digital currency derivatives trading market also has the potential to contribute to the transformation of trading markets. LedgerX and TeraExchange will be among the world's first fully regulated financial markets built upon digital currency technologies and communities. The models they provide for the financial industry can have a profound and long-lasting future impact. Both of these initiatives serve to mark an important transition in the development of virtual currency systems.

Matsuura Chapter 7:
Appropriate Regulatory Oversight for Digital Currency as a Commodity

CHAPTER 7

Appropriate Regulatory Oversight for Digital Currency as a Commodity

Abstract: Virtual currencies are bought and sold in digital markets in the same manner as other goods, subject to traditional laws governing contracts, commercial sales, and consumer protection. Those currencies are also used as the basis for financial products including future contracts and other financial derivatives. When digital currency is traded as a financial product and when digital currency platforms are used to create and operate financial markets, the currency and its platforms are subject to the oversight of financial regulators. This dual nature of legal compliance associated with virtual currency and its platforms is essential. Under these circumstances, digital currency systems and activities face different legal compliance challenges depending on their specific functions. Understanding this environment is essential for effective legal compliance in the virtual currency community.

Keywords: CFTC, contracts, exchanges, LedgerX, markets, TeraExchange, trades.

When traded as a commodity, digital currency is subject to the oversight of traditional commodities trading regulatory authorities. That oversight extends to the parties involved in the trades, the markets and other intermediaries that help to facilitate the transactions, and the exchanges and other marketplaces where the transactions take place. Commodity trading oversight generally focuses on the trades involving the financial derivatives, such as future contracts, associated with the underlying commodity. Direct purchases of basic commodities, agricultural products for instance, are generally regulated by laws associated with contracts and commercial sales. In contrast, transactions involving future contracts and other forms of derivatives built upon the commodities receive special commodities trading regulatory oversight. This same legal framework is applicable to virtual currencies.

Direct use of digital currency in commercial transactions does not result in commodities trading oversight. When a consumer purchases goods or services using digital currency, that transaction is a traditional commercial sale, not a commodity trade. Even when a buyer purchases bitcoin or other digital currency, that transaction is viewed to be either a commercial sale or a currency conversion, not a commodities trade. However, when a buyer purchases the right to buy or sell digital currency at a specific price by a specific future date, that transaction is a

Jeffrey H. Matsuura
All rights reserved-© 2016 Bentham Science Publishers

commodities trade and it is subject to the regulatory oversight of the authorities tasked with protecting the integrity of future markets.

Digital currencies are presently traded as commodities through a variety of trading exchanges. The popularity of those transactions is likely to increase in popularity, particularly given the volatility of market prices for bitcoin and other digital currencies. The highly volatile digital currency valuations make future contracts and other financial derivatives attractive as a method for managing risk.

The evolution currently in progress with regard to derivatives trading for virtual currencies is the regulatory formalization of the markets that process that trading. As noted previously, operations such as LedgerX and TeraExchange are pursuing full regulatory approval for their derivatives trading markets. They are seeking approval from relevant authorities, including the CFTC. Once operational, those exchanges recognize that they will operate subject to the oversight of the financial services regulators. The trading process associated with virtual currencies as commodities and with the trading of digital currency-based derivatives is presently becoming incorporated into the existing regulatory regime associated with commodities and derivatives. This process strongly suggests that, although virtual currency platforms seem likely to transform substantially markets for commodities and derivatives, they will do so subject to the oversight of traditional regulatory authorities applying traditional regulations. Virtual currency systems and technologies may have a major impact on commodities markets in the future, but their operations will most likely remain entirely subject to conventional regulatory oversight. Markets operating through use of virtual currency technologies continue to provide services and to process financial transactions that are conventional and governed by well-established regulatory frameworks. In this environment, it is entirely appropriate for those unconventional markets to be overseen by traditional financial regulators applying existing regulatory requirements.

CHAPTER 8

Overview of Securities Regulation

Abstract: Securities are a range of financial instruments including stocks, bonds, and derivatives. They represent funding provided by investors to enable third parties to operate businesses for profit. Owners of securities do not perform the work of operating the business, but instead provide funds necessary for the business and receive financial return from the business for their investment. Securities are governed by an active and extensive set of regulations around the world. Under some circumstances, virtual currencies fall within the regulatory oversight of securities regulators. The primary goal of securities regulation is protection of the integrity of the investments and markets associated with all securities.

Keywords: Bonds, financial instruments, securities, stocks.

Financial instruments known as securities provide evidence documenting the existence of legally binding and enforceable ownership or debt. For example, stock issued by enterprises to their owners serves as evidence of their ownership interest. Similarly, bonds issued by businesses provide proof of the existence of binding debt. Securities are the instruments that serve as proof of the existence of a financial obligation. Under certain circumstances, virtual currencies are considered to be regulated securities.

Securities regulation commonly focuses on protection of the integrity of the investment process. For example, in the United States, registration and other regulatory obligations associated with securities apply to a range of investment activities. Although there is often a tendency to focus on publicly traded stocks as securities, a far broader range of investment vehicles are also subject to regulation as securities.

Securities regulation in the United States and other jurisdictions is applied to investment activities that have certain critical characteristics [92]. All such activities involve investment of money into a common enterprise, a single entity or operation. That enterprise must be established with the intent of deriving profits and the profits associated with the enterprise must arise solely from the efforts of parties other than the investor. To qualify as a form of regulated security, there must be a financial investment, with the intention of deriving economic gain, in some type of commercial activity conducted by parties other than the investor. In the world of securities, investors are not directly in control of the decisions and activities associated with the underlying business.

Jeffrey H. Matsuura
All rights reserved-© 2016 Bentham Science Publishers

Securities regulation is structured and applied in a manner intended to protect the interests of securities holders. By protecting those interests, regulators create and maintain an environment that makes potential investors and lenders confident as to the integrity and safety of securities transactions. Preservation of the integrity of the marketplaces in which securities transactions are processed is essential to maintenance of the confidence of marketplace users. That user confidence is essential in order to sustain effective securities investments.

CHAPTER 9

Digital Currencies as Securities and Their Impact on Regulation

Abstract: Digital currency can be applied in ways that subject the currency to regulatory oversight as financial securities. Digital currency platforms can be used to support and operate electronic trading exchanges for the sale and purchase of financial securities. This dual nature of virtual currency systems subjects those systems to multiple levels of regulatory oversight. To the extent that digital currency is used as a security, it is subject to traditional securities regulation. When virtual currency platforms operate to enable securities trading, they are subject to regulatory oversight as securities trading exchanges. The dual nature of digital currency systems substantially increases the scope and complexity of legal compliance efforts.

Keywords: Australia, crypto-stocks, cyber-securities, electronically traded funds, exchange traded notes, Finland, Ireland, Israel, Overstock.com, Project Medici, securities, Securities and Exchange Commission, stocks, Sweden, trading exchange.

Given the broad definition of securities applied in various jurisdictions, it is entirely possible for digital currency transactions and operations to fall within the scope of securities regulation. Virtual currency platforms support a range of financial investment opportunities that can qualify as securities. For example, individuals are already provided with the opportunity to invest in electronically traded funds that own bitcoin as a financial investment. ETFs are treated as securities for regulatory purposes, and ETFs specializing in bitcoin investment are no different, they are subject to the oversight of securities regulators.

Digital currencies seem to confuse traditional regulatory authorities. The actions of regulators in different parts of the world seem to reflect uncertainty as to how best to characterize digital currencies for oversight purposes. For instance, the Finish Tax Authority issued initial guidelines regarding tax treatment for digital currencies in Finland [93]. Those guidelines indicate that Finish capital gains tax rules are applicable when digital currencies are sold or converted to another currency. The Finish authority also interpreted its tax rules and concluded that losses incurred upon the sale of digital currency holdings are not tax deductible. These interpretations do not seem to reflect a clear and consistent definition of the status of digital currencies in Finland for tax purposes. Finish tax authorities do not yet seem to know for sure how best to define and characterize digital currency

Jeffrey H. Matsuura
All rights reserved-© 2016 Bentham Science Publishers

as a financial instrument. This confusion appears to be shared by governments around the world.

The Israel Tax Authority asserts that virtual currency trading profits are taxable [94]. However, the precise tax approach applicable to those profits in Israel remains unclear. The Israeli approach seems to be a common one. Tax authorities in a variety of jurisdictions seem quick to claim tax jurisdiction over virtual currency transactions, but slow to describe the specific terms of that tax liability. The Central Bank of Ireland seems to view virtual currency activities as an extension of traditional commercial activities and transactions for tax purposes [95].

Australian regulators currently take the position that digital currencies are not securities or other financial product. The Australian Securities and Investments Commission (ASIC) determined that digital currencies are not financial products [96]. Accordingly, parties who sell, buy or hold digital currencies are not subject to Australian financial products licensing requirements. The ASIC also suggested, however, that licenses and other traditional regulatory oversight may be applicable when the services involved include some form of interaction between the digital currency and traditional financial products or services. This suggests for example, that certain transactions involving conversion of digital currency into traditional currency could, depending on their specific terms, constitute a future contract or a form of financial derivative, thus subject to existing ASIC requirements.

Digital currency operations are also subject to oversight by securities regulators to the extent that digital currency platforms support the operations of digital trading exchanges. Digital currency can be regulated securities and it can also operate as a regulated securities trading exchange. Both functions subject the digital currency and its platform to oversight by securities regulators. Note for example, that the company, Overstock.com, is working to develop a securities trading exchange that is intended to operate using the Bitcoin digital currency platform [97]. Overstock's "Project Medici" is being designed to provide an automated platform to process the issuance and trading of securities, and that platform will operate using the software, network, and community that have developed to support the Bitcoin digital currency system.

When evaluating digital currency use, from the perspective of financial securities, it is important to recognize that they can be both the traded securities and the exchange platform over which securities are traded. In both capacities, the digital currencies are subject to the established regulatory framework applicable to financial securities. This dual nature makes digital currencies particularly special, from a financial regulatory perspective. The dual nature also means that virtual currency platforms supporting securities transactions will likely be subject to two levels of regulation, the first associated with the securities traded through the platform and the second based on the platform's operation as a trading exchange.

As efforts establish securities trading exchanges built upon digital currency platforms such as bitcoin evolve, those initiatives will be subject to existing securities trading and markets regulation. For instance, Overstock's Project Medici is developing within the context of Securities and Exchange Commission requirements for securities trading and the markets that process those trades. Overstock has requested authority from the SEC to continue its Project Medici exchange development efforts [98]. Through Project Medici, Overstock is reportedly exploring the possibility of issuing "cyber-securities" [99]. Cyber-securities would make use of the distributed cryptographic platform to create a blockchain ledger documenting and executing stock trades. Instead of a traditional stock exchange, the Project Medici model would handle stock trades through use of a blockchain-based transaction ledger. Presumably, all of the trades processed through the blockchain would involve use of the digital currencies supported by the platform.

Digital currency systems also affect traditional securities trading be making those currencies accessible to investors through established securities markets and investment vehicles. Authorities in Sweden have, for example, authorized creation and trading of exchange traded notes (ETNs) that invest in bitcoin [100]. Through this ETN, investors will be able participate in the bitcoin ecosystem without buying of holding bitcoin directly. Instead, those investors will purchase interests in the ETN which will, in turn, buy, sell, and hold bitcoin. Through this process, digital currency is, in effect, another investment option accessible to investors through existing securities trading marketplaces. As bitcoin and other forms of digital currency are at present unfamiliar to most investors, the ETN process provides an effective mechanism for the average investor to participate in the virtual currency marketplace with a significantly reduced exposure to risk.

Crypto-currency platforms also provide a forum through which crowd-funding can be used to provide financial backing for enterprises and specific projects. Operations such as Crypto:Stocks enable investors to fund activities through bitcoin and other digital currency payments [101]. These systems are not operating as formal securities markets, however, they do provide sources of capital for businesses, the same function which is at the heart of traditional securities markets. As these crowd-funding applications for virtual currency systems mature, there is likely to be increasing regulatory attention to their activities.

Digital currencies are commonly used as financial instruments that qualify for traditional regulatory oversight. The virtual currency platforms developed by Bitcoin and other digital currency developers are now also used as electronic platforms that support and process securities trades. Virtual currency is thus, depending on specific applications and circumstances, subject to regulatory oversight both as actual financial securities and as the markets or trading exchanges in which securities and other financial products are bought and sold. This dual nature of virtual currencies and their operating platforms substantially enhances the challenges associated with legal compliance in the context of securities regulation.

CHAPTER 10

Effective Integration of Digital Currencies and Traditional Securities Regulation

Abstract: Securities regulators around the world are examining the extent to which digital currency activities and platforms are within the scope of their jurisdiction. Most regulators take the position that the extent of their oversight authority is entirely dependent on the actual functional activities of the digital currency system operations. In some jurisdictions, digital currency operations deemed to be electronic services or financial product offerings are subject to oversight. Key participants in the virtual currency community, such as Overstock.com and LedgerX, are increasingly taking the position that they will pursue full compliance with existing regulatory requirements to the extent that their digital currency operations fall within the scope of existing regulation. This approach is prudent and likely to facilitate growth of the virtual currency market. The approach does, however, require extensive legal compliance activity.

Keywords: Australia, California, China, Denmark, electronic services, financial products, financial services, fraud, LedgerX, New York, Overstock.com, Ponzi scheme, Securities and Exchange Commission, Shavers case.

Parties involved in the creation and use of digital currencies must remain mindful of the unsettled relationship between those currencies and traditional securities regulation. As noted previously, digital currencies may fall within the scope of traditional securities regulation to the extent that the transactions and operations associated with those currencies are consistent with traditional definitions of securities. Some of the formats and applications for digital currency platforms may cause those platforms and the activities they support to be recognized by regulators as securities, subject to oversight.

An important component of securities regulation is its focus on the integrity of the transactions and markets in which securities are exchanged. Protection of this integrity is essential in order to provide the public with the confidence necessary for their continuing participation in securities investments. National regulatory authorities such as the Securities and Exchange Commission in the United States oversee the markets, market transactions, and market participants.

In addition to regulatory oversight of digital currencies as securities, some jurisdictions consider the process of creating, distributing, and converting digital currencies to be forms of financial services. In virtually every nation, certain

Jeffrey H. Matsuura
All rights reserved-© 2016 Bentham Science Publishers

financial services are subject to regulatory oversight. Such oversight generally includes registration and licensing of service providers, as well as continuing regulation of the conduct of those service providers. Thus for example, bankers and banking institutions, as well as stock brokers and brokerage firms are commonly subject to regulation as a result of the financial services they provide.

In jurisdictions where various activities associated with the creation, distribution, and use of digital currencies are deemed to be financial services, those services are likely to be subjected to some forms of regulatory oversight. Some governmental authorities, those in California and New York in the United States for example, appear to be moving toward characterization of at least some activities associated with digital currency creation, distribution, and use as regulated financial services. In contrast however, other authorities such as the Financial Supervisory Authority (Finanstilsynet) in Denmark specifically acknowledge that digital currency is not a financial service, thus it is presumably not subject to traditional financial services regulation [102].

The Danish approach to digital currency raises other law and policy issues, however. Although the authorities in Denmark have to date chosen not to characterize digital currency operations as financial services, their apparent classification of digital currency activities as electronic services will likely have different legal implications. As electronic services, digital currency operations will apparently be subject to the legal obligations associated with digital and online services in Denmark. Additionally, as commercial services in Denmark, presumably earnings from those operations will be subject to Danish income tax obligations.

Other jurisdictions apply a framework of regulations to sale of financial products. Australia, for instance, requires licensing and ongoing oversight for parties who sell financial products to the public. The Australian Securities and Investments Commission (ASIC) has regulatory jurisdiction over financial products. At present, the ASIC takes the position that digital currencies are not financial products. This classification means that parties that facilitate the creation, storage, and use of digital currencies generally do not require ASIC licenses [103]. The ASIC has determined, however, that digital currency services that enable digital currencies to interact with traditional financial products (*e.g.*, services that convert digital currencies to traditional currency or other traditional financial products) may require ASIC licensing based on their connection to traditional, regulated financial products.

A key focus of regulation of securities markets and trading is protection of the integrity of securities transactions. Regulatory authorities emphasize the importance of preventing fraud in securities trading. Government entities responsible for preventing securities fraud are currently active in the virtual currency environment. For example, the Securities and Exchange Commission (SEC) in the United States has conducted highly visible prosecutions alleging securities fraud in the digital currency system. The SEC charged Trendon Shavers, creator and operator of the Bitcoin Savings and Trust with violation of U.S. securities laws, alleging that he used a Ponzi scheme process to defraud investors [104]. According to the SEC, Shavers offered outrageously high interest payments to potential investors to attract them to provide funds for purchase of bitcoin. After purchasing approximately 764,000 bitcoin, authorities contend that Shavers misappropriated approximately 140,000 bitcoin [105]. The authorities allege that Shavers used funds provided by new investors to compensate previous investors, thus making the process a classic Ponzi scheme.

The SEC took action in this case based on its interpretation that the contracts between Shavers and the bitcoin buyers were financial securities regulated by the SEC. the federal court handling the Shavers case agreed with the SEC. It concluded that Shavers had violated U.S. securities laws by engaging in conduct that deceived and defrauded investors and by offering securities for sale without prior registration with the SEC. The court order Shavers to disgorge more than $40 million in funds he had acquired through the fraudulent conduct [106]. This case provides an important precedent in the United States for regulatory action by the SEC under U.S. securities laws when virtual currency brokers engage in fraudulent conduct with respect to potential or actual investors. The SEC continues to warn the public of the potential for securities fraud in the virtual currency environment through notices and alerts [107].

The Shavers case signals the willingness by the SEC to treat agreements to invest in digital currency purchases as a form of securities investment. Based on that interpretation, the SEC asserted jurisdiction over those investment transactions in order to prevent fraud. It seems likely that other securities regulators in different jurisdictions may adopt a similar approach, asserting their own jurisdiction over digital currency investment activities to prevent fraud. Assertion of authority by securities regulators also seems to indicate that parties engaging in digital currency brokerage activities for investors will be subject to the registration and reporting requirements enforced by securities regulators in conjunction with securities transactions. This issue could prove to be significant as it would subject virtual currency brokers to a substantial range of securities regulation already in existence.

Authorities are also facing legal enforcement challenges associated with fake virtual currency trading exchanges. Authorities in China, for instance, recently began prosecution of individuals who allegedly established and operated a fake bitcoin trading exchange in China. The fake exchange reportedly had more than 4,000 registered users and allegedly caused a loss to those users of approximately 25 million yuan [108].

The efforts by Overstock.com to create a securities trading exchange operating exclusively upon the cryptographically secured distributed ledger platform pioneered by Bitcoin and other digital currencies could have a major impact on securities trading and the regulation of that trading in the future. In 2015, Overstock filed a prospectus with the United States Securities and Exchange Commission seeking regulatory authority to launch and operate Overstock's alternative trading system (ATS) for digital securities [109]. The ATS proposed by Overstock would initially support sale of up to $500 million in stock and other forms of securities. Under this authorization, Overstock would in effect create an entirely digital securities trading environment, free from the traditional intermediaries such as clearinghouses and other entities that have processed securities transactions in the past.

The Overstock proposal reportedly anticipates ultimately processing transactions involving all forms of securities, not only traditional stocks [110]. The entire operation of the exchange would function as a cryptographically secure distributed ledger software system, intended to bring with it the benefits of end user empowerment, increased operating efficiency, and transactional transparency [111]. Proponents of use of digital currency platforms and technologies in support of securities trading contend that those systems will be more transparent for users and regulators, less costly, and more efficient than traditional trading exchanges. Overstock recently purchased a stake in a registered traditional securities broker-dealer company, and some observers suggest that this investment could be part of the preparation for the actual launch of the new exchange, in anticipation of ultimate SEC approval [112].

Overstock's efforts to develop and launch its innovative securities trading exchange on a technology platform pioneered by Bitcoin and other virtual currency systems offers an important lesson for the overall expansion and diversification of digital currency platform applications. By electing to pursue and obtain SEC approval of its new exchange, Overstock is helping to set an extremely useful precedent both for the global digital currency community and for governments. Overstock is acting in a manner consistent with existing laws, policies, and regulations governing securities trading. Although its plan is highly innovative, makes use of new technologies, and has the potential to transform dramatically securities trading around the world.

Overstock chose to abide by all relevant existing laws and regulations applicable to its proposed securities trading activities. It did not attempt to argue that the existing legal framework was not applicable to its innovative system, but opted instead to pursue all existing regulatory approvals appropriate for the operational functions and activities it intends to pursue, despite that fact that its plan will conduct those operations and activities in an extraordinarily unconventional manner and could result in fundamental transformation of the securities trading environment. It is important to recognize this process as it is likely that a rapidly growing number of diverse applications for virtual currency platforms and technologies will emerge. As each of these new and innovative applications develop, they are likely to require approvals and to submit to regulatory oversight from traditional governmental authorities. Overstock's approach of identifying and systematically pursuing all such necessary approvals and clearances provides an excellent model for the developers of other applications that will apply the blockchain and other digital currency system technologies.

Overstock's proposed offering parallels the effort underway by LedgerX in the context of derivatives trading. While LedgerX is moving to apply the cryptographically-based distributed computing network platform to derivatives trading, Overstock seeks to apply that same platform to the full range of securities trading. If successful, the two initiatives have the potential to transform financial market operation. Their experiences can verify the feasibility of distributed computing network use for sophisticated financial trading exchanges. If successful, they will likely pave the way for additional cryptographically-based distributed computing networks operating financial exchanges.

Proponents of use of cryptographically-based distributed computing platforms for securities markets contend that those systems can actually enhance the integrity of the markets involved. Those technologies make the transactions processed by the market more transparent for both users of the market and for regulators. Additionally, the systems reduce the role of intermediaries in the trading environment, thus bringing buyers and sellers closer together in more direct transactions, which should reduce operating costs and the risks of errors and misconduct.

Financial regulators around the world are currently in the process of determining best practices for the application of their existing jurisdiction to both the transactions processed by cryptographically-based distributed computing networks and the overall use of those networks as trading exchanges. This dual nature of regulatory involvement in use of virtual currency platforms for securities trading is perhaps the most critical and fascinating aspect of securities regulation in the digital currency environment. This challenge is likely to keep securities regulators and digital currency exchange operators busy well into the future.

CHAPTER 11

Regulation of Digital Currency Businesses and Platforms

Abstract: An increasing number of jurisdictions, such as New York, California, and the Isle of Man are developing legal initiatives specifically directed toward digital currency. Many other jurisdictions are modifying their existing laws to more clearly and specifically address digital currency and its applications. Even in jurisdictions where such initiatives are not underway, digital currency is already subject to an extensive and complex set of legal compliance obligations established by existing laws, including contract, commercial transactions, criminal, property, and consumer protection requirements. Virtually every category of law already has influence over virtual currencies and their use. Legal compliance efforts are already necessary for all members of the digital currency community, ranging from casual users all the way through the more active members of the global virtual currency community. In the world of digital currency, legal compliance is a vital and complicated challenge which is already present and demands immediate attention.

Keywords: Antitrust, arbitration, BitLicense, Bitstamp, Butterfly Labs, commercial transactions, consumer complaints, Consumer Financial Protection Bureau, criminal law, disclaimers, escrow, Federal Trade Commission, fraud, insurance, intermediaries, liability limits, Mt. Gox, smart contracts, theft, trusted platforms.

A rapidly developing regulatory trend associated with digital currency use involves oversight of the businesses that make use of digital currency value exchange platforms. These regulatory regimes are generally not directed at businesses that accept digital currency as a form of payment, but instead apply to enterprises that are directly involved in the digital currency creation, storage, conversion, and trading activities. Authorities appear to be increasingly interested in exercising oversight over the businesses and other organizations that facilitate and process digital currency transactions. It is important to recognize that oversight is being applied through both development of new legal requirements directed specifically toward virtual currency operations and through application of existing business law obligations to the new operating contexts presented by digital currency systems and operations.

For example, the State of New York is in the process of enacting a regulatory framework that will require certain digital currency businesses to obtain a license from the New York Department of Financial Services prior to commencing operations [113]. The proposed New York digital currency system does not require

Jeffrey H. Matsuura
All rights reserved-© 2016 Bentham Science Publishers

licensing of businesses that accept digital currency payments. Instead, it requires organizations involved in the following activities to obtain a license: 1.) transmission or storage of digital currency for customers; 2.) buying and/or selling of digital currency on behalf of customers; 3.) issuing, administering or controlling digital currency for customer, 4.) performing digital currency conversions for customers [114]. This New York "BitLicense" process requires that digital currency operations covered by the requirements must implement and maintain procedures that ensure consumer protection and cybersecurity, while also complying with all relevant anti-money laundering and know-your-customer obligations. The New York BitLicense program became operational in June 2015 [115].

The New York legal initiative for digital currency illustrates both the increasing emphasis on new rules specifically aimed at virtual currency business operations and the application of existing business laws to digital currency activities. The BitLicense program in New York is a new regulatory initiative inspired almost entirely by the rise of virtual currency platforms. The actual implementation of those new rules is, however, the responsibility of the traditional financial service regulators in New York. The New York effort is thus a digital currency focused program, but its operational structure is integrated into the existing, well-established framework for the regulation of financial services in New York.

The State of California is considering a similar licensing framework for digital currency businesses [116]. As is the case in New York, the proposed legislation in California is not directed toward businesses that accept digital currency as a form of payment or parties who make payments in digital currency form. The legislation does not focus on the parties who create, mine, virtual currency. Instead, it is intended to regulate enterprises that provide services associated with the transmission, storage, and conversion of digital currency. Also like the New York effort, the California initiative would integrate oversight of digital currency activities into the existing financial services regulatory framework already in operation in California.

To the extent that authorities are considering regulatory oversight specifically directed toward the virtual currency ecosystem, the attention seems to focus on storage (*e.g.*, wallet), brokerage, and conversion activities. Intermediaries who assist parties to purchase, sell, or manage virtual currency holdings are increasingly viewed to be providing financial services of the kind that are traditionally subject to government regulation. For instance, the government of the United Kingdom is presently reviewing recommendations that it apply regulatory oversight similar to that applied to banks to parties who provide digital currency wallet services. This approach would, in effect, treat virtual currency storage accounts as bank accounts, requiring that the providers of those services implement record-keeping and due diligence procedures to ensure that they can effectively identify and locate their customers [117]. This regulatory approach would include requirements of government authorization for the wallet service providers and ongoing compliance with government-established rules.

In contrast to the recommendation now under consideration in the United Kingdom regarding regulation of virtual currency wallet functions, other governments appear to be less eager to exercise such oversight. For instance, a recent report issued by the Canadian Senate adopts a different stance with respect to digital currency wallets. The Committee on Banking, Trade, and Commerce of the Canadian Senate recommended that regulation of digital currency exchanges under money transmission rules was appropriate, but also suggested that virtual currency wallet services should, for the present, remain unregulated [118]. It is important to recognize, however, that even if certain virtual currency support functions remain outside the scope of specific regulations, their will continue to be legal compliance obligations associated with those activities.

Consider digital currency storage, wallet services for example. Even if the Canadian government abides by its Senate's suggestion that wallet services remain free from specific regulatory oversight, a significant network of legal requirements will continue to be applicable to those services in Canada. Contract terms and conditions binding the users and providers of the wallet services will continue to govern those relationships. Similarly, Canadian consumer protection rules will likely be applied to the interaction between wallets service operators and their customers. All parties involved with the development of virtual currency systems should remain mindful of the fact that an extensive pre-existing set of laws and regulations are applicable to the operations of those systems even absent creation of new legal requirements specifically directed toward the digital currency activities.

Another increasingly important set of intermediaries playing a key role in the virtual currency ecosystem are parties who provide escrow services. The escrow process involves use of trusted third parties as part of commercial transactions. Two parties to a transaction commonly use the escrow process in which trusted third parties hold payments and property until all conditions associated with the final closing of the transactions are met. The escrow process reduces the risk of non-performance by one of the parties and it provides assurance to the parties that they will not bear costs associated with a failure to perform by another party. The escrow process is well-established and widely used for a variety of commercial transactions and activities. Escrow services are commonly provided by parties operating under special licensing or ethical obligations such as lawyers and financial service providers.

Escrow service providers are increasingly popular for virtual currency transactions [119]. As those transactions are irrevocable and frequently involve numerous pre-conditions, parties using digital currencies now often employ escrow service providers. The escrow function is an important one in support of virtual currency transactions. Active escrow support can provide extremely valuable assistance to the security and effectiveness of the virtual currency marketplace. As a result of this important role, it seems likely that authorities may soon direct oversight attention directly toward escrow service providers. Virtual currency escrow service providers may soon be included among the intermediaries in the digital currency marketplace subject to specific regulatory review. Regulators may soon implement registration, reporting, and bonding requirements for parties seeking to provide virtual currency escrow services. Given the critical nature of escrow services, it is also likely that escrow service providers will soon face legal liability for transactions they mediate which are not fully executed as anticipated by the parties. Escrow service providers involved in virtual currency transactions face a set of legal compliance obligations which is already complex and is likely to become even more complex in the near future.

In the context of digital currency systems, escrow service providers are sometimes characterized as trust platform providers. An example of this type of operation is the Bitrated platform [120]. Another example of this trusted platform process is provided by Multisig [121]. Trusted platforms basically perform escrow functions, but they often become more directly involved in transactions than do traditional escrow service providers. Trusted platforms frequently insert themselves directly into the transactions they support, interacting directly with all parties to the transactions. In this way, they essentially become direct parties to the transactions, not merely guarantors or referees of the transactions of other parties. Functioning in the broader role of trust platform operators, escrow service providers will face even more complex legal compliance challenges.

In addition to facilitating the direct processing of transactions, trusted platforms also provide other services to improve the integrity of the transactions they support. For instance, trusted platforms can retain records of the reputations of parties using the platform. Based on that data, the trusted platforms can provide ratings documenting the trustworthiness of parties, ratings which provide useful information for other parties considering conducting business with the rated individuals. Trust platforms have an important role to play in the digital currency ecosystem. By serving as transaction processing platforms, they increase the volume of digital currency-based commerce. By helping to make virtual currency transactions more trustworthy and reliable, they encourage grater use of digital currencies in the commercial environment.

As noted previously, the government of Brazil has enacted legislation that authorizes use of a broad range of digital currency systems. The Brazilian law recognizes a wide range of electronic currencies. It defines electronic currency as essentially any electronic payment system. This approach seems to be one of the most expansive government strategies for digital currencies, and it can have noteworthy implications. By defining electronic currency broadly, the Brazilian law extends its policymaking focus beyond Bitcoin and other current forms of digital currency. It links current digital currencies with the many other current electronic payment platforms, such as credit and debit cards. The law also connects digital currencies with other electronic payment platforms such as PayPal, and with new payment systems which will emerge in the future.

Some advocates and observers of digital currency initiatives speak in terms of regulation of digital currency. When governments do not enact legislation or rules specifically targeting digital currency creation, distribution or use, there is often a tendency to take the position that digital currency has not been regulated. Although this may technically be true, it is also very misleading. It is misleading because even without legal oversight specifically aimed at digital currency and its use, several different existing sets of laws and regulation have profound impact on the development and evolution of digital currency. Digital currencies of all forms in all jurisdictions must operate within the existing framework of laws and regulations applicable to commercial relationships, operations, and transactions.

Providers of digital currency services must, for instance, comply with laws prohibiting fraud. Efforts to deceive or mislead individuals and organizations in the course of commercial interactions can result in criminal and civil law violations to the extent that they are determined to constitute fraud. Legal prohibitions against fraud are applicable to all virtual currency ecosystems, despite the fact that they have not been specifically modified to address the digital currency environment. Compliance with laws and regulations against fraud is mandatory for all parties, including those involved with virtual currencies, even without initiatives that specifically apply those legal requirements to the virtual currency environment.

There have already been a variety of legal actions taken in jurisdictions around the world in response to allegations of digital currency fraud. Many of these legal enforcement actions have been taken without any new laws applying anti-fraud provisions to the virtual currency context. Authorities recognize that the digital currency marketplace is particularly open to questionable trading practices such as the "pump and dump" process where currency owners spread false or misleading rumors in an effort to attract buyers, thus raising the market price for the currency at which time they sell their holdings at the higher price. This approach has, at times, been applied in the bitcoin marketplace [122].

Parties engaged in the sale of their digital currency holdings have been the targets of fraud and theft. In the United Kingdom, for example, parties attempting to sell bitcoin through online auction systems such as eBay have been the target of fraudulent purchases in which apparent buyers placed orders for the bitcoin, made electronic payment, received the purchased bitcoin in wallets specified by the apparent buyers, then rescinded the payments but retained the bitcoin. It appears that these fraudulent purchases involved payments made through hacked PayPal and other accounts. The bitcoin purchase orders and payments were apparently made by hackers using payment accounts of third parties without authorization. The actual owners of those payment accounts not surprisingly rescinded the payments as they had not actually placed the purchase orders. The policies of the electronic payment processes protect the owners of the hacked payment accounts from liability, however, the policies of the online auction systems do not always, apparently, protect the good faith sellers of the bitcoin. Those sellers thus potentially face liability to the payment processing systems and the online auction systems as a result of the fraudulent sales, a result which seems patently unfair [123].

Fraud continues to be a major legal issue facing virtual currency systems in all jurisdictions. The scope of the problem is substantial and at times even involves fraudulent conduct by government authorities. For example, two federal law enforcement agents in the United States were charged under federal wire fraud and other criminal laws as a result of their conduct during the investigation of the Silk Road online market. The agents are alleged to have engaged in fraud and theft as they apparently made use of their knowledge of the investigation to gain access to substantial bitcoin holdings for personal gain [124]. The risk of fraud associated with virtual currency system extends beyond the parties directly involved in digital currency transactions and relationships. It also extends to the parties who regulate and enforce legal requirements in the digital currency economy.

The challenges to the virtual community posed by fraud are significant enough that they attract substantial attention from virtual currency advocates. For instance, the Bitcoin Association of Hong Kong actively encourages potential bitcoin users to seek comprehensive information about the bitcoin platform and to be skeptical of claims associated with profits and potential future value of bitcoin holdings. In effect, the Association is cultivating development of an informed community of bitcoin users, and it reminds potential bitcoin community members that they have the ability to participate directly by mining bitcoin and not relying solely on the services provided by bitcoin intermediaries [125]. The virtual currency community is acutely aware of the fact that the threat of fraud presents one of the most serious threats to the future growth of digital currency applications.

A related yet distinct legal challenge associated with virtual currency us is the problem of theft. The intangible and global nature of digital currencies makes them highly attract targets for thieves. Digital currency exchanges face continuing security challenges as they attempt to protect themselves from theft. Their virtual nature make the marketplaces where digital currencies are bought and sold highly attractive targets for thieves. Authorities around the world continue to highlight to the public the potential security risks associated with virtual currency use and the fact that essentially all of those risks fall upon the users of those securities. For instance, the Reserve Bank of India underscored to the public its concerns about the ongoing security risks associated with digital currency use [126].

Perhaps the most notorious recent example of large-scale theft involving virtual currency is the case of the Mt. Gox bitcoin exchange. At one point, Mt. Gox was one of the world's largest and most active markets for bitcoin. Its prominence made Mt. Gox an attractive target for thieves. Over the course of years, thieves apparently managed to steal approximately 850,000 bitcoins from the exchange, as well as millions of dollars from the exchange's bank accounts [127]. The large-scale theft fundamentally undermined the stability of Mt. Gox, and the exchange entered bankruptcy proceedings in 2014.

Mt. Gox is not the only example of the serious threat posed to virtual currency exchanges by thieves. Another exchange, Bitstamp, was reportedly the victim of thieves who apparently stole approximately 19,000 bitcoins from the exchange [128]. The thefts resulted in suspension of Bitstamp services, as the thefts undermined the integrity of the Bitstamp system. Theft remains a major challenge facing all virtual currency exchanges.

Note that the problem of virtual currency theft is a challenge for the marketplace where the currency is bought and sold. The underlying integrity of the digital currency platforms involved, Bitcoin in the case of Mt. Gox and Bitstamp, remains intact. To date the burden of theft is felt by the exchanges that process purchases of virtual currencies and the wallets used to store digital currency holdings. The fundamental mining process through which Bitcoin is issued has not been threatened.

Security threats in the virtual currency environment make insurance an increasingly attractive option. The world of digital currency insurance coverage is currently only beginning to emerge. Among the first parties to obtain such coverage are some of the wallet, storage service providers. The specific terms of that coverage remain unclear, however, it has been reported for example that Elliptic, a provider of bitcoin storage services apparently obtained coverage from insurer Lloyd's of London for the currency it stores on behalf of clients at a rate believed to be approximately two percent of the value of the insured bitcoin holdings [129].

Other virtual currency storage systems are also moving toward more extensive use of insurance coverage to protect themselves and their clients. For example, digital currency storage service provider, Xapo, indicates that it provides insurance coverage for the currency holdings it manages [130]. Some form of insurance is likely to be a basic component of virtual currency storage and other services in the not too distant future.

Depending on the terms of coverage, insurance can provide a useful risk mitigation strategy for parties involved in the virtual currency environment. If experience in the cybersecurity insurance context is a guide, however, the digital currency insurance market is likely to be unsettled and uncertain for a substantial period of time. Parties providing insurance for the virtual currency community will most likely be subject to the existing regulatory oversight framework that currently governs insurance providers and the coverage they offer. As a more standardized structure for virtual currency insurance emerges, expect the rates associated with such coverage to be high in the early days and the terms of coverage to be extremely limited, as insurers attempt to enter the market while simultaneously minimizing their risks in the unsettled, rapidly evolving, and highly dynamic virtual currency environment.

Even without specific new laws addressing digital currency and its use, the well established and comprehensive rules applied to protection of consumers are applicable to businesses operating throughout the digital currency ecosystem. Consumer protection laws are generally structured to protect individual consumers from predatory, deceptive, and unfair business practices. All of those existing protections apply to digital currency businesses, even without modifications to those rules specifically identifying their applicability to digital currency businesses. Consumer protection authorities around the world already have the ability to monitor and regulate digital currency activities through their jurisdiction over commercial operations. Legal compliance associated with existing consumer protection rules is likely to be among the most active topics of focus for the global virtual currency community.

For instance, an enterprise offering digital currency storage (wallet) services to consumers is expected to comply with all relevant laws and regulations designed to protect consumers from false or misleading advertising. Consumer protection authorities such as the Federal Trade Commission in the United States are now extremely active with regard to preserving the privacy personal information associated with consumers, thus all digital currency businesses are expected to protect such information from security breaches and unreasonable commercial use. These requirements are now actively enforced against all businesses, and that enforcement extends to digital currency business operations, even without development of new rules specifically directed toward digital currency business operations.

Consumer protection regulations are likely to be particularly significant in the context of digital currency use as average consumers may frequently be confused and unsettled as to digital currency system practices and use. Expect enforcement of general consumer protection requirements for digital currency use to expand significantly in the near future. Requirements associated with clear and reasonable business practices and full disclosure of threats and risks are almost certain to be among the most actively applied consumer protection measures in the context of digital currency.

Regulatory approaches evolving in different jurisdictions help to illustrate the framework of consumer protection oversight likely to be applied to digital currency products and services in the future. Those requirements seem to focus on the financial stability and scope of the digital currency businesses, their ability to provide effective and adequate security for their products and services, and the transparency of their business operations to permit effective review and oversight by government authorities and the public.

Emerging best practices for consumer protection in the context of digital currency service and product providers include several fundamental topics. Consumer protection requirements included in the proposed digital currency business licensing system of the State of New York illustrate the key components of consumer protection in the digital currency environment [131]. The New York proposal requires documentation of consumer protection policies, practices, and procedures and effective notice of those protective measures to the public. It requires meaningful disclosure of potential risks to consumers. It also requires documentation of complaints and errors, and of the ultimate resolution of those complaints and errors.

The New York approach also requires that digital currency businesses retain actual digital currency holdings in trust for customers. This requirement of some level of held digital currency reserves solely for the benefit of customers is an important requirement which is likely to be adopted by other jurisdictions, over time. The New York oversight framework also requires digital currency businesses to obtain surety bonds and to disclose the effective levels of insurance coverage maintained by the businesses.

Even without legislation or regulation directed specifically toward digital currency businesses and activities, participants in the digital currency ecosystem must comply with a wide range of legal requirements. In addition to consumer protection rules, digital currency initiatives and transactions will also be subject to antitrust and competition law obligations. Competition law enforces basic requirements associated with open and fair commercial competition. It prohibits, for example, unreasonable discrimination as to prices, access to goods and services, and terms of service. Competition law also prohibits actions collusion and other actions intended to reduce or block fair commercial competition in markets. These fundamental provisions and principles of competition law are relevant to digital currency operations, transactions, and relationships, and they are likely to incite important and diverse enforcement actions in the context of digital currency systems, products, and services.

An interesting potential context for issues of antitrust and competition law in the context of virtual currencies may at some point involve the compatibility of different digital currencies, their platforms, and the support services associated with them. At present, Bitcoin is the most widely used and recognized digital currency system. There are, however, a variety of other virtual currencies currently in use. It is possible that at some future point competition law conflicts could emerge as competing digital currency systems attempt to grow and cultivate competitive advantage. For example, Bitcoin has arguably established itself, at present, as the dominant provider of digital currency. If Bitcoin, in fact, successfully establishes dominance in the global virtual currency market, it could be the target of future antitrust actions in the event that others at some point claim that Bitcoin has abused its dominant position in order to impede competition or competitors. If for example intermediaries such as wallet service providers and trading exchanges were to collude with the Bitcoin platform operators to block or impede the development of alternative virtual currencies, those activities could constitute violations of antitrust and competition laws. There have of course been no such antitrust or competition law claims raised in the virtual currency marketplace, however, those laws are applicable to that marketplace just as they apply in conventional competitive commercial markets.

Another critical set of legal obligations affecting digital currency development is the law of contracts and commercial transactions. Contact and commercial transactions law is well established and routinely governs the global network of commercial relationships and arrangements. These rules are of vital importance to the expansion and evolution of digital currencies. These laws define the form of commercial arrangements which are enforceable by the legal system. They are critical to the effectiveness of the digital currency ecosystem. Only if the diverse transactions involving digital currencies are legally enforceable will digital currencies provide a viable economic value exchange platform.

Although the financial activities of digital currencies and their associated markets and transactions have profound global regulatory implications, perhaps the most significant aspect of digital currency, from a legal and public policy perspective, results from its potential to serve as an international platform enabling a wide range of commercial operations that extend beyond traditional financial markets. Digital currency sector observers note that the true power of crypto-currency systems such as Bitcoin is their ability to develop and sustain global communities involved in a virtually limitless array of commercial activities and initiatives. The process of exchanging economic value was the first application for the cryptographically-based distributed computing networks established by Bitcoin and others, but we now see that many other applications, some with the potential for significant commercial value, can also be efficiently and effectively performed by those networks. As those additional applications for the virtual currency networks become more widely deployed, the range of legal compliance challenges facing the parties involved will increase dramatically.

The algorithms, computer programs, and communities of users that enable crypto-currency systems such as Bitcoin to develop and operate now serve as platforms to support an ever-expanding ser of commercial relationships and activities in addition to the economic value exchange functions offered by the original digital currency applications. The platforms offered by Bitcoin and other crypto-currency systems enable creation, operation, and management of distributed cryptographic transaction ledger systems that are global in nature and which permit all nodes in the network to share the transaction history information accumulated over time. The most valuable capability of the distributed cryptographic networks which were first developed to facilitate payments and the exchange of economic value is the ability of those networks to create permanent, publicly accessible records documenting all transactions executed through the system [132]. Those permanent records are accessible to all users of the platform and can not be deleted, hidden or altered by any party. Thus the core capability of these networks is their ability to provide a trusted, complete, and readily accessible history of all of the activities executed using the network. That core capability has numerous potential applications with commercial significance that extends beyond the economic value exchange capability.

A variety of service providers have created commercial communities that are built and operate upon the Bitcoin platform [133]. Bitmessage provides communications services that make use of the secure, distributed, and transparent platform provided by Bitcoin [134]. Namecoin makes use of the Bitcoin platform to support Internet domain name management operations [135]. Ethereum builds on the Bitcoin platform to offer a system for commercial contract validation and enforcement [136]. All of the various applications that use the platforms provided by Bitcoin and other crypto-currency networks use those platforms to support and sustain services and operations that are decentralized, secure, transparent, and are operated by their communities of users.

The range of applications performed by distributed cryptographic networks continues to expand and the number of parties providing those services grows daily. For example, Counterparty uses a distributed cryptographic network to enable parties to develop, maintain, and enforce a range of commercial contracts involving financial relationships and transactions [137]. Factom assists businesses to develop and maintain permanent records associated with data which verify and document time and content, a framework which can facilitate future auditing and dispute resolution for many different types of business data including commercial billing and payment information [138].

The evolving nature and applications associated with Bitcoin and other crypto-currency platforms indicate that the ultimate significance of these systems is likely to extend far beyond the scope of traditional financial activities such as currency, payment, and financial investments. The most significant long-term impact of digital currency systems is likely to be their growing future role as the platforms that enable and sustain a virtually limitless set of applications that are used and managed by a de-centralized community of users. The key public policy, legal, and regulatory challenges associated with the rise and diversification of these self-managing commercial communities will involve the development of mechanisms that provide for effective enforcement of key legal principles in those self-managing communities.

Perhaps the most critical aspects of the operational systems made possible by digital currency platforms are their de-centralized nature and their transparency. The platforms offered by Bitcoin and other crypto-currency systems eliminate the operational need for a central authority, and they provide all users with direct access to all transactional and other functional details associated with the activities supported by the systems. Each member of the community created by the platform is empowered by direct access to critical information and by the ability to participate in the application supported by the platform directly, without the intervention of an intermediary party.

Although these platforms eliminate the operational need for an intermediary authority, they do not necessarily provide an alternative for the moderating and dispute resolution functions of traditional community intermediaries. The fact that all participants to transactions can access key information directly and that the network enables direct decision-making and action by each community member will not eliminate disputes or misunderstandings involving transaction parties. The virtual currency platforms are not organized in a manner that provides for effective dispute and conflict resolution. The continuing challenge presented to the developers of crypto-currency communities and to governments is the need to ensure that public interest concerns are effectively incorporated into the structure and operations of the digital communities.

Critical legal and regulatory issues emerge at each point where the platforms that facilitate the applications managed by the distributed communities encounter traditional organizations, transactions, and processes. For example, when the virtual currencies that support transactions processed by the platform are converted into traditional currencies, there is an encounter between the virtual community and established institutions and processes. When there is a dispute associated with a self-enforcing contract enabled by a platform such as Ethereum, the parties involved in that dispute will likely turn to traditional legal institutions and processes to resolve it. Self-enforcing or "smart" contracts made possible by virtual currency networks are not capable of resolving all disputes or disagreements. Participants in these virtual currency systems will continue to make use of courts and other dispute resolutions forums even when their transactions are governed by self-enforcing contracts.

There are contractual relationships binding all participants in the virtual communities associated with digital currencies and distributed cryptographic systems, in general. All users of those systems must agree to abide by the terms associated with system use. All operators of the platforms that support the virtual communities and all providers of services and applications that are supported by the platforms must offer and agree to be legally bound by reasonable terms of use and service. These contractual commitments can take the form of formal written contracts, terms of use, licenses, and other legally enforceable instruments. These contractual commitments provide a basic framework of legal oversight for all virtual communities. These commitments are legally enforceable and provide a baseline of legal order for the distributed communities, even if governments do not enact laws or regulations specifically directed toward these virtual communities.

It is likely that there will be a great deal of legal activity in the near future associated with interpretation and enforcement of the contracts that define the terms and conditions associated with virtual currency use and the development of diverse applications provided through use of virtual currency platforms and communities. It is reasonable to expect that this activity will be similar to that which has evolved in the context of website use, electronic commerce transactions, digital media applications, and social media communities. In each of these contexts, agreements between service providers and users, often characterized as terms of use or terms of service, have provided the primary legal framework for defining rights and obligations for the providers and users of digital content and services. It is reasonable to assume that there will be similar emphasis on service contracts in the context of digital currency platforms and communities.

Essentially all parties involved in the virtual currency ecosystem already rely substantially on terms of service and other contractual arrangements to establish the rights and obligations of both service providers and users. A common approach in the digital currency community is for service providers to attempt to avoid as much potential legal liability as is feasible. For example, the Bitcoin platform essentially asserts that it disclaims all liability for harm to users caused by user error, technical problems or failures, security breaches, and actions of third parties [139]. This approach is also commonly applied in the broader online and e-commerce communities and it has consistently been the source of substantial public policy controversy.

The developers, owners, and operators of digital services, platforms, and communities have every incentive to seek to avoid or substantially limit their responsibility for negative consequences of their offerings. This effort to avoid legal liability for adverse consequences of digital activities has been a clear trend through the development of the Internet and its associated operations. That trend seems to be extending into the virtual currency communities, where the providers of the various products, services, and technologies necessary for the development and use of digital currency communities all seem to avoid or place severe limits on their level of legal responsibility for any adverse consequences resulting from their offerings.

Liability limits are imposed through contracts. Those contracts often take the form of standard terms of service, terms of use or service agreements which users are required to accept in order to access the digital currency products, services, or platforms. These contracts are intended to be legally enforceable promises that establish the rights and obligations of the parties involved in the transaction or relationship. In effect, these contracts create a legal framework to govern conduct as the parties perform the agreed upon activities. Up to a point, courts and other legal authorities permit parties involved in commercial activities to agree upon limitations on legal liability. When however, those agreements are viewed to be unfair or unreasonable, authorities are willing to set those terms aside and impose instead provisions that are more reasonable and fair for all parties.

A framework of legal responsibility imposed and enforced by private contracts can result in a fair and effective commercial operating environment, but only if all of the parties participating in those agreements have equal bargaining power. This means that all of the parties to be bound by the contracts must have adequate knowledge, experience, resources, and economic leverage to ensure that the contracts are truly the result of fair negotiation between parties with comparable commercial power. Authorities traditionally recognize and assume the existence of equal bargaining power when two businesses of comparable size and experience are involved. When one of the parties to the agreement is an individual consumer, however, governments generally assume that the bargaining power of the parties is not balanced. Instead, when individual consumers are involved, authorities generally assume that the commercial enterprise has the advantage over the individual consumer, and thus has the power to shape the contract terms in its favor, often to the detriment of the consumer.

The terms of commercial contracts between businesses and their individual customers can be challenged by the customers to the extent that they appear to place the consumers in an unreasonably disadvantaged position. Although commercial enterprises commonly establish contract terms that are substantially biased in their favor, to the disadvantage of consumers, those terms are not always enforced by legal authorities. If courts, regulatory agencies, and other government authorities determine that contract terms are unreasonably unfair to individual consumers, they will refuse to enforce those provisions.

Efforts by businesses to limit their potential legal liability resulting from harm their goods or services cause to consumers are common in virtually all sectors of business. E-commerce businesses, for example, are widely known to include severe liability limits in their contracts with consumers. As the Bitcoin legal disclaimer illustrates, this practice appears to be popular with businesses involved with digital currency, as well. It seems likely that there will be substantial debate in the near future regarding the extent to which efforts by digital currency companies to avoid or limit their liability for damages their products and services cause to consumers will become increasingly active. It also seems reasonable to assume that the level of these debates will soon increase to a level where it will attract the attention of consumer protection agencies and other regulatory authorities tasked with protecting the integrity of commercial transactions.

Numerous virtual currency service providers attempt to place significant limits on their potential legal liability through contract terms. For instance, digital currency trading exchange operator TeraExchange disclaims liability for all of its actions except those involving gross negligence, fraud, and willful misconduct, while also requiring that all legal claims against it must be brought within one year from the date when the claim arose, regardless of when the customer first became ware of the existence of the claim [140]. Bitcoin storage service provider Flexcoin disclaims all liability associated with coins that are lost by the customer, under any circumstances [141].

Experience in e-commerce highlights another flashpoint for consumer contract terms. E-commerce businesses have widely adopted the practice of mandatory arbitration for all dispute resolution. These companies routinely include in their terms of service and other service agreements with consumers the requirement that all disputes the consumer may have with the company must be resolve through arbitration instead of the courts. Bitcoin has also adopted this strategy, as reflected in its Legal Disclaimer [142]. Digital asset trading exchange, Kraken, also requires its customers to submit to mandatory arbitration for dispute resolution and to waive their rights to litigate [143]. Similarly, wallet and conversion services provider, Coinbase, requires its customers to submit to binding arbitration for dispute resolution [144].

Commercial companies often prefer arbitration for dispute resolution as they generally believe that arbitrators and arbitration forums are frequently more favorable to commercial interests than to individual consumers. Mandatory arbitration also enables businesses to reduce the risk and uncertainty associated with litigation in courts in numerous jurisdictions which are often subject to wide discrepancies in results due in large part to the wide variety of jurors and judges involved.

Mandatory arbitration is frequently, however, more difficult for individual consumer to manage effectively. A requirement that consumers turn only to arbitration to address their disputes with a company can force consumers to relinquish their ability to take action against the business in a court in their home jurisdiction. This process often places the consumer at a serious disadvantage relative to the business involved. It can cause consumers to hesitate to raise complaints and can thus discourage individuals from enforcing their legitimate rights.

Consumer protection authorities and courts are aware of the business preference for mandatory arbitration, and they are willing to override that provision under circumstances where consumers can demonstrate that the provision is unreasonably unfair to customers. The issue of mandatory arbitration for resolution of consumer disputes is an increasingly significant issue in e-commerce in general, and will likely become significant in the virtual currency community, as well. In this environment, businesses in the digital currency sector should approach efforts to require arbitration for consumer dispute resolution cautiously. Users of digital currency platforms and products should be mindful of this issue and in the event that disputes arise, they should explore the possibility of turning to regulatory authorities or the courts to seek relief from the arbitration requirement.

Another common focus of contracts associated with virtual currency platforms and services is notice of risk. Virtual currency platforms, such as Bitcoin, attempt to use their service agreements as a vehicle to notify users as to the risks associated with use of virtual currencies. The agreements highlight the known risks and indicate that users are assuming those risks fully be electing to participate in the digital currency community. Providers of digital currency products and services appear to be most concerned about liability arising from failures in the operation of their platforms, such as security breaches. They also seem to be concerned that users of their systems understand that digital currencies are highly volatile with respect to their economic value and that a variety of taxes may apply to digital currency transactions. Legal disclaimers presented by Bitcoin and other digital currency service providers highlight these particular risks, apparently in an effort to ensure that users appreciate their implications.

Experience in e-commerce suggests that issues associated with effective notice to consumers are significant and have a major impact on allocation of legal rights and obligations. The key challenge associated with notice to consumers is providing mechanisms to ensure that consumers have easy access to information that is critical to their commercial decision-making. In the e-commerce context, important issues regarding risks associated with information privacy and the security of data and transactions must be communicated effectively to consumers, and the processes used by businesses to describe those issues effectively to consumers have been subject to substantial scrutiny by legal authorities.

The various digital currency platforms and associated commercial ecosystems are novel and currently still emerging. This environment, at least for the near-term future, presents important challenges as to provision of adequate information to individual consumers to enable them to make informed judgments regarding their use of digital currency and their participation in the communities associated with digital currency. Individual participants in virtual currency communities must, from a consumer rights perspective, be provided with adequate knowledge as to the risks associated with their participation in those communities to ensure that their decision to participate is a reasonably informed one and that their acceptance of the risks is meaningful.

Term of service and other customer contracts in the e-commerce environment routinely include notices intended to document informed consent by individual consumers. There continues to be debate and discussion as to what precisely constitutes informed consent in the e-commerce environment, particularly with regard to topics associated with assumption of risk by the consumer. It is virtually certain that controversy as to effective notice and informed consent involving digital currency users will emerge as a significant legal topic in the near future.

As has been the case in e-commerce, the setting in which the debate over effective notice and informed consent will likely first take place in the digital currency environment will be through legal actions involving consumer contracts associated with goods and services. As individual consumers are harmed as a result of their participation in virtual currency platforms, through security breaches resulting in loss of their digital currency holdings for example, they will likely seek recourse through traditional legal actions such as breach of contract lawsuits. Their claims will likely include the contention that the digital currency businesses involved did not provide comprehensive, accurate, and understandable notice as to the risks associated with digital currency use.

As the claims from consumers increase in number, consumer regulatory authorities, such as the Federal Trade Commission at the national level in the United States and the various state consumer protection authorities operating in virtually all fifty states will likely take action monitoring the risk disclosures made by digital currency businesses. Government consumer protection agencies generally have broad authority to take action against activities perceived to be unfair to consumers. Disputes as to the required level and form of notice to consumers using digital currency platforms will almost surely become widespread in the very near future, and many of those disputes will find their way to the FTC and other consumer protection authorities.

The FTC is playing an increasingly active role in consumer protection in the digital currency marketplace. For example, as more consumer transactions make use of Bitcoin and other virtual currencies, the number of consumer complaints involving those currencies grows. The FTC recently launched a consumer blog providing advice to consumers who use digital currency in their transactions [145]. Among the most frequent consumer complaints involving purchases using digital currencies are failure of product delivery and merchant insistence on refunds in store credits instead of currency [146]. The FTC notes that failure of product fulfillment and mandatory store credits for refunds are the leading issues raised by consumers using digital currencies.

It is important to note that these particular complaints are not unique to digital currencies. Consumer frustration as to failure to deliver purchased products on time is present in sales involving all forms of payment. Similarly, consumers using all forms of payment raise complaints when the merchants involved insist on providing refunds only in store credits. As consumer protection issues receive greater attention, it is essential that we recognize which of those issues are unique to the virtual currency marketplace and which are present in all forms of consumer transactions. It seems somewhat unfair for the FTC and other consumer protection organizations to highlight as digital currency consumer risks issues and threats that are, in reality, present in all forms of consumer sales, not only those involving digital currencies. To be sure, there are certain risks that are likely to present greater threats when digital currencies are used, however, it seems that the vast majority of risks facing consumers are present no matter what form of payment is used, and they are definitely not unique to the virtual currency marketplace.

The FTC also took enforcement action against a company that failed to provide promised high-speed computers it had marketed for use in the digital currency mining process. Butterfly Labs sold thousands of dollars worth of computers it claimed could effectively engage in the bitcoin mining process, a process requiring sophisticated computing capability applied to resolving complex algorithms in order to earn new bitcoins. The FTC claims that Butterfly Labs failed to provide many of the computers it sold and delivered other computers far later than promised, resulting in substantial economic harm to the equipment buyers. The FTC persuaded a U.S. federal court to order Butterfly Labs to cease its operations and to begin the process of compensating the customers involved for their losses [147].

The Butterfly Labs case is important as it present one of the first examples of consumer regulatory action based on virtual currency activities more complex than the simple use of those currencies in commercial transactions. In the Butterfly Labs situation, the consumers involved were parties who intended to participate in the bitcoin mining process. They thought they were purchasing sophisticated computing equipment specifically designed to function effectively in the bitcoin mining process. The failure of Butterfly Labs to deliver the products it promised prevented the customers from engaging in the commercial enterprise of bitcoin mining, and the actions of Butterfly Labs were judged to be sufficiently unreasonable as to constitute illegal abuse of consumers.

The Butterfly Labs case suggests that legal liability could also arise in the context of the operational failure of computing equipment and software. Authorities acted against Butterfly Labs because it failed to deliver promised computing equipment. Liability can also exist in some jurisdictions if hardware or software fails to perform consistent with promised standards. For example, if digital currency mining software is technically flawed and thus fails to perform as promised, the provider of the software could face legal liability for breach of contract or for sale of faulty products. In some jurisdictions, the developers of the software could face tort law liability under a form of products liability claim to the extent that the product flaws were the result of some form of negligent or malicious conduct and the flaws resulted in harm to product users or to third parties.

In the United States, the Consumer Financial Protection Bureau (CFPB), the federal regulatory agency tasked with the duty of protecting consumers as they engage in financial activities, now plays an increasingly visible and active role in the virtual currency ecosystem. The CFPB has issued guidance to consumers with regard to use of digital currencies [148]. To date, the CFPB's efforts have focused on fostering greater consumer knowledge of the opportunities and risks presented by digital currencies. In the future, CFPB involvement with virtual currencies will likely include development and enforcement of rules applicable to those currencies and activity as an arbitrator of disputes between consumers and various digital currency service providers. The CFPB proposed new rules providing for more extensive and specific oversight of pre-paid financial products, and it indicated that those new rules would likely be applicable to virtual currencies [149].

The CFPB is already prepared to handle consumer complaints associated with digital currencies. The online complaint process offered by the CFPB specifically identifies virtual currencies as a complaint category, included with money transfer complaints [150]. Under the CFPB complaint process, consumers can file their complaints online, and the CFPB commits to processing of the complaint within sixty days. The CFPB complaint process is likely to present an active mechanism for addressing consumer complaints arising from digital currency use. It may well provide the clearest indication of the extent to which digital currencies are already well within the scope of consumer protection oversight.

Accordingly, these virtual communities and the applications that they operate do not function beyond the reach of established laws and regulations. Distributed cryptographic data networks are platforms for commercial transactions and interaction. As commercial platforms, they are subject to the full range of existing commercial and consumer laws even if those laws are not specifically adjusted to address virtual communities directly. Thus even at this early stage of development for the virtual communities operating on distributed cryptographic computer networks, a robust and relatively extensive legal framework is in place to govern development and use of those networks, despite the fact that few jurisdictions have yet enacted rules and regulations directly aimed at those networks.

The existing laws of contracts and commercial transactions are relevant and enforceable as to the rights and obligations of operators and users of the virtual communities and associated services. Consumer protection laws are applicable to the relationships and interaction between the operators of cryptographic distributed platforms and their users. Rights and obligations imposed by antitrust and competition law are applicable to the business practices engaged in by operators of virtual communities and the providers of the services and applications associated with those communities. Finally, laws and regulations governing traditional specialized activities (*e.g.*, securities and commodity trading, currency conversion, and taxation) are applicable to the activities of distributed cryptographic platforms whenever those platforms directly engage in the regulated conduct.

In addition to the complex network of established civil laws that are already applicable to virtual currency creation, distribution, and use, there is an equally complicated global network of criminal laws that affect virtual currencies. Perhaps the most significant example of existing criminal laws engaging with digital currencies is the framework of computer and data security laws now in place in many different jurisdictions around the world. Criminal laws similar to the Computer Fraud and Abuse Act in effect at the federal level in the United States have been enacted in many different countries and regional jurisdictions [151]. In general, these laws impose criminal sanctions such as monetary fines and prison terms when there are violations of the security and integrity of computers, computer systems, and computer content.

These computer and data security laws generally have scope sufficient to address a variety of activities involving virtual currency development and use. As digital currencies are, in effect, entirely creations of computer operations and they are distributed, stored, and used exclusively through computers and computer networks, virtually all activities associated with digital currencies are within the scope of standard computer security and data protection laws. This condition has major implications for the future of virtual currencies.

At present, few jurisdictions have yet enacted laws, rules or regulations specifically addressing development and use of these virtual platforms. Yet, those platforms are already subject to significant legal compliance obligations arising out of existing laws that address the current applications of those platforms and the parties who use the platforms. Virtual currency communities are currently establishing and enforcing their own sets of rights and obligations. The most common vehicle for creating and managing those rights and obligations is contract law. In the near future however, as the scope of activity for virtual currency communities and platforms expands, an extremely wide range of government authorities will play active roles in oversight of digital currency systems and activities.

All individuals and organizations involved in transactions and activities using digital currencies as well as those considering future use of those currencies must monitor and understand the global framework of rights and obligations which affects the virtual currency community. They must monitor and understand that setting in order to identify and protect their commercial and legal interests. In addition, that knowledge is vital if they are to comply with their obligations of due diligence and reasonable care.

Current experience in the world of cybersecurity clearly illustrates that business owners, employees, contractors, suppliers, and customers all face some level of obligation to be aware of, and to develop a basic level of understanding of, the computer and data security legal and regulatory issues facing their organizations. That knowledge is required in order for the individuals involved to satisfy their due diligence and reasonable care obligations owed to their organizations and their business partners. A similar environment is emerging in the context of virtual currency. Just as management of a business is now required to develop a basic level of fluency and understanding as to computer and data security activities, threats, and risks, so too will management, in the near future, be required to develop comparable understanding of digital currency use.

It is now widely recognized that virtual currency platforms and systems have important potential value for nations, individuals, businesses, and other organizations. Prior to active use of those currencies and associated platforms and systems, it is vital, however, that the parties involved effectively complete their due diligence review of the opportunities and risks associated with virtual currency use by their organizations. Part of that due diligence is development of an understanding of the legal rights and obligations associated with participation in the virtual currency ecosystem. In order to exercise satisfactorily their obligation of reasonable care for the organizations with which they are affiliated, individuals must thoroughly consider the legal and regulatory implications of digital currency use by their organizations.

Identification and evaluation of legal and regulatory issues associated with digital currency use must be an integral part of each organization's decision-making process as it considers the extent to which it will make use of virtual currencies and the platforms with which they are associated. Failure to understand, review, and evaluate legal rights and obligations associated with digital currency use prior to a decision to make use of that currency is a failure to meet clearly established obligations of due diligence and reasonable care. Such review is admittedly extremely challenging, at present, due to the nascent, unclear, and incomplete nature of the digital currency oversight activities of governments and other applicable authorities. Yet despite this difficulty, there is without a doubt a current obligation to consider legal and regulatory aspects of digital currency use as strategies for digital currency are developed and implemented.

Even as new laws and regulations specifically directed toward the various potential applications of virtual currency platforms emerge, there is already in place an extensive and global set of legal obligations with which all members of the digital currency must comply. Those laws include the legal requirements associated with commercial contracts and transactions. They also include consumer protection rules and the obligations associated with securities, financial instruments, and property. The elaborate framework of tax laws in diverse jurisdictions is applicable to digital currency, as is the well-established set of criminal laws. As we have seen, virtually every existing field of law is applicable in some form, under some circumstances, to the operational platforms and user communities that are developing in the cryptographically-based distributed computing network environment. Those networks enable and support a wide range of commercial applications extending far beyond the basic economic value exchange they were originally designed to support. The wide and ever-expanding range of their applications continues to increase the scope and complexity of the legal compliance challenges they encounter.

Legal compliance associated with the virtual currency community is already a significant major issue for a wide range of individuals and organizations. The scope and complexity of that issue will continue to grow rapidly for the foreseeable future. This book provides a stating point for the development of effective legal compliance strategies appropriate for the digital currency environment. The work of effectively establishing, updating, managing, and implementing those strategies has only just begun.

REFERENCES

REFERENCES

[1] Internet Document, Financial Action Task Force, "Guidance for a Risk-Based Approach to Virtual Currencies" Appendix B, 2015 [Online]. Available: www.fatf.org/media/fatf/documents/reports/Guidance-RBA-Virtual-Currencies.pdf [Accessed: 26th June 2015].

[2] Internet Document, European Central Bank, "Virtual currency schemes – a further analysis", 2015 [Online]/ Available: www.ecb.europa.eu/pub/pdf/other/virtualcurrencyschemes.pdf [Accessed 6th April 2015].

[3] Internet Document, Litecoin, "Litecoin", 2015 [Online]. Available: https://litecoin.org [Accessed: 15th May 2015].

[4] Internet Document, No Author Given, "Government Needs to Make Bitcoin Regulation", 2013 [Online]. Available: http://economy.hankocki.com/page/economy/201312/e2013122715412370070.htm [Accessed 5th January 2014].

[5] Internet Document, No Author Given, "Written Question and Answer No. 5-8723 to Belgium Finance Minister, Martine Tuelman", Apr. 16, 2013 [Online]. Available: www.senate.be/www/?Mlval=/index_senate&MENUID=23100&LANE=fr (search by question number) [Accessed: 3rd September 2013].

[6] Internet Document, No Author Given, "Law No. 12,865 of Oct. 9, 2013", 2013 [Online]. Available: www.receita.fazenda.gov.br/Legislacao/leis/2013/lei/2865.htm [Accessed: 15th December 2013].

[7] Internet Document, No Author Given, Notice on Precautions Against the Risks of Bitcoins", 2013 [Online]. Available: www.pbc.gov.cn/publish/goutongjiaoliu/524/2013/10131205153156832222251/20131205153156832 222%20251.html and https://vip.btcchina.com/page/bocnotice2013 [Accessed: 10th January 2014].

[8] Internet Document, United States Treasury Department, "Legal Tender", 2014 [Online]. Available: www.treasury.gov/resource-center/faqs/Currency/Pages/legal-tender.aspx [Accessed: 28th March 2015].

[9] Internet Document, Reserve Bank of New Zealand, "Notes and Coins Frequently Asked Questions", 2013 [Online]. Available: www.rbnz.govt.nz/notes_and_coins/0094941.html [Accessed: 5th January 2014].

[10] Internet Document, No Author Given, "Resmi Gazete No. 6493,28690", 2013 [Online]. Available: www.resmigazete.gov.tr/eskiler/2013/06/20130627-14.htm [Accessed: 15th August 2013].

[11] Internet Document, European Central Bank, "Virtual currency schemes – a further analysis", 2014 [Online]. Available: www.ecb.europa.eu/pub/pdf/other/virtualcurrencyschemesen.pdf [Accessed: 1st March 2015].

[12] Internet Document, David George-Cosh, "Canada Says Bitcoin Isn't Legal Tender", 2014 [Online]. Available: http://blogs.wsj.com/canadarealtime/2014/01/16/canada-says-bitcoin-isnt-legal-tender [Accessed 20th January 2014].

[13] Internet Document, Ministry of Finance of the Netherlands, "Answers to Parliamentary Questions on the use and Control of New Digital Means of Payment Such as Bitcoin", 2013 [Online]. Available: www.rijksoverheid.nl/onderwerpen/betalingen-en-beleggingsverzekeringen/docymenten-en-publicaties/kamerstukken/2013/12/19/beantwoording-kamervragen-over-het-gebruik-van-en-toezicht-op-nieuwe-digitale-betaalmidden-zoals-de-bitcoin.html [Accessed: 2nd January 2014].

[14] Internet Document, Banque de France, "The Dangers of the Development of Virtual Currencies: The Bitcoin Example" 2013 [Online]. Available: www.banque-france-fr/fileadmin/user_upload/banque_de_france/publications/Focus-10-stabilite-financiere.pdf [Accessed: 15th December 2013].

[15] Internet Document, Bank Indonesia, "Statement of Bank Indonesia Related to Bitcoin and Other Virtual Currency", 2013 [Online]. Available: www.bi.go.id/en/ruang-media/siaran-pers/Pages/SP_160614.aspx [Accessed: 15th February 2014].

[16]   Internet Document, Michael Lee, "Singapore Issues Tax Guidance on Bitcoins", 2013 [Online]. Available: www.zdnet.com/singapore-issues-tax-guidance-on-bitcoins-7000024966 [Accessed: 9th January 2014].

[17]   Internet Document, Everett Rosenfeld, "Ecuador becomes first country to roll out its own digital cash", 2015 [Online]. Available: www.cnbc.com/id/102397137 [Accessed:4th May 2015].

[18]   Internet Document, No Author Given, "Ecuador's e-Money Initiative Outlaws Bitcoin, Makes Mandatory for Banks to Follow Dictate", 2015 [Online]. Available: http://insidebitcoins.com/news/ecuadors-e-money-initiative-outlaws-bitcoin-makes-mandatory-for-banks-to-follow-dictate/33058 [Accessed: 11th June 2015].

[19]   Internet Document, Stan Higgins, "Ecuador Bans Bitcoin, Plans Own Digital Money", 2015 [Online]. Available: www.coindesk.com/ecuador-bans-bitcoin-legislative-vote [Accessed: 15th June 2015].

[20]   Internet Document, Tanaya Machael, "The Case for Merging Mexico's Peson With Block Chain Technology", 2014 [Online]. Available: www.coindesk.com/case-merging-mexicos-peso-block-chain-technology [Accessed: 26th July 2014].

[21]   Internet Document, Franz Nestler, "Germany Recognizes Bitcoins as Private Money", 2013 [Online]. Available: www.faz.net/aktuell/finanzen/devisen-rohstoffe/digitale-waehrung-deutschland-ekennt-bitcoins-als-privates-gold-an-12535059.html [Accessed: 29th August 2013].

[22]   Internet Document, Reserve Bank of India, "RBI Cautions Users of Virtual Currencies Against Risks", 2013 [Online]. Available http://rbi.org.in/scripts/BS_PressReleaseDisplay.aspx?prid=30247 [Accessed: 15th January 2014].

[23]   Internet Document, No Author Given, "First Time in the Country, ED Raids Bitcoin Seller in Ahmedabad", 2013 [Online]. Available: www.dnaindia.com/india/report-first-time-in-the-country-ed-raids-a-bitcoin-seller-in-ahmedabad-1941187 [Accessed: 16th January 2014].

[24]   Internet Document, No Author Given, "Croatian Central Bank Establishes that Bitcoin is Legal in Croatia", 2013 [Online]. Available: www.reddit.com/r/Bitcoin/comments/1sjgby/croatian_central_bank_establishes_that_bitcoin_is [Accessed: 15th January 2014].

[25]   Internet Document, No Author Given, "Bitcoin Trading Illegal in Iceland According to Icelandic Central Bank", 2013 [Online]. Available: www.reddit.com/r/Bitcoin/comments/1t8zf3/bitcoin_trading_illegal_in_iceland_according_to/ [Accessed: 9th January 2014].

[26]   Internet Document, Daniel Palmer, "Bank of Thailand Suggests Bitcoin Not Illegal But Warns Against Its Use but Warns Against It Use", 2014 [Online]. Available: www.coindesk.com/bank-thailand-says-bitcoin-ullegal-warns-use [Accessed: 14th June 2015].

[27]   Internet Document, Jake Maxwell Watts, "Thailand's Bitcoin Ban is not Quite What It Seems", 2013 [Online]. Available: http://qz.com/110164/thailands-infamous-bitcoin-crackdown-is-not-quite-what-it-seems [Accessed: 31st July 2013].

[28]   2015. Internet Document, No Author Given, "Vietnam says bitcoin transactions are illegal", 2015 [Online]. Available: http://phys.org/news/2014-02-vietnam-bitcoin-transactions-illegal.html [Accessed: 11th June 2015].

[29]   Internet Document, Pete Rizzo, "Bolivia's Central Bank Bans Bitcoin", 2015 [Online] Available: www.coindesk.com/bolivias-central-bank-bans-bitcoin-digital-currencies [Accessed: 15th June 2015].

[30]   Internet Document, No Author Given, "Notice on Precautions Against the Risks of Bitcoins", 2013 [Online]. Available: https://vip.btcchina.com/page/bocnotice2013 [Accessed: 10th January 2014]

[31]   Internet Document, Allen Scott, "Russia Bitcoin Ban Expected in August; Expert Recommends Businesses 'Get Out'", 2015 [Online]. Available: www.cointelegraph.com/news/113857/russias-bitcoin-ban-expected-in-august-expert-recommends-businesses-get-out [Accessed: 15th June 2015].

[32]   Internet Document, Pete Rizzo, "Kyrgyzstan: Bitcoin Payments Violate State Law", 2015 [Online]. Available: www.coindesk.com/krgyzstan-bitcoin-payments-violate-state-law [Accessed: 13th June 2015].

[33]   Internet Document, No Author Given, "Cyprus Central Bank Warns About Risks in Use of Bitcoin", 2013 [Online]. Available: http://famaugusta-gazette.com/cyprus-bank-warns-about-risks-in-use-of-bitcoin-p21892-69.htm [Accessed 20th December 2013].

[34]   Internet Document, No Author Given, "Law No. 12,865 of Oct. 9, 2013", 2013 [Online]. Available: www.receita.fazenda.gov.br/Legislacao/leis/2013/lei/2865.htm [Accessed: 15th December 2013].

References

[35] Internet Document, European Central Bank, "Virtual currency schemes – a further analysis", 2015 [Online]. Available: www.ecb.europa.eu/pub/pdf/other/virtualcurrencyschemesen.pdf [Accessed: 29th April 2015].

[36] Internet Document, Charles Casar, "Malta Bitcoin Company", 2013 [Online]. Available: www.ccmalta.com/publications/malta_bitcoin_company [Accessed: 8th January 2014].

[37] Internet Document, Banque de France, "The Dangers of the Development of Virtual Currencies: The Bitcoin Example", 2013 [Online]. Available: www.banque-france.fr/fileadmin/user_upload/banque-de-france/publications/Focus-/0-stabilite-financiere.pdf [Accessed: 5th December 2013].

[38] INTERNET DOCUMENT, European Parliament, "EU Directive 2009/110/EC of the European Parliament and of the Council of 16 September 2009 on the Taking Up, Pursuit, and Prudential Supervision of the Business of Electronic Money Institutions, Amending Directives 2005/60/EC and 2006/48/EC, 2009", 2009 [Online]. Available: http://eur-lex.europa.eu/LexUriServ/LexUriServ.do?uri=OJ:L:2009:267:0007:0017:EN:PDF and INTERNET DOCUMENT, European Parliament, "EU Directive 2007/64/EC of the European Parliament and of the Council of 13 November 2007 on Payment Services in the Internal Market, Amending Directives 97/7/EC, 2002/65/EC, 2005/60/EC, and 2006/48/EC, and Repealing Directive 97/5/EC, 2007", 2009 [Online]. Available: http://eur-lex.europa.eu/LexUriServ/LexUriServ.do?uri=OJ:L:2007:319:0001:0036:EN:PDF [Accessed:2nd December 2013].

[39] Internet Document, Cade Metz, "NY Backs Bitcoin Exchange But It May Not Fly in California", 2015 [Online]. Available: www.wired.com/2015/05/new-york-backs-bitcoin-exchange-may-not-fly-california [Accessed: 10th May 2015].

[40] Internet Document, Grace Caffyn, "Isle of Man Trials First Government-Run Blockchain Project", 2015 [Online]. Available: www.coindesk.com/isle-of-man-trials-first-government-run-blockchain-project [Accessed: 10th May 2015].

[41] 2015. [Online]. Available Internet Document, NO AUTHOR GIVEN, "Getcredits", 2015 [Online]. Available: http://getcredits.io [Accessed: 10th May 2015].

[42] Internet Document, Canadian Parliament, Canadian Senate Committee on Banking, Trade, and Commerce, "Digital Currency: You Can't Flip This Coin!" 2015 [Online]. Available: www.parl.gc.ca/Content/SEN/Committee/412/banc/rep/rep12jun15-e.pdf [Accessed: 22nd June 2015].

[43] Internet Document, Robert McMillan, "Instead of Fighting Bitcoin, the US Could Make Its Own Digital Currency", 2015 [Online]. Available: www.wired.com/2014/12/t-coin [Accessed: 27th May 2015].

[44] Internet Document, Rosalind McLymont, "Digital Currency: A Leapfrog Moment for Africa", 2015 [Online]. Available: www.africastrictlybusiness.com/news-analysis/digital-currency-leapfrog-moment-africa [Accessed: 4th June 2015].

[45] Internet Document, European Central Bank, "Virtual currency schemes – a further analysis", 2015 [Online]. Available: www.ecb.europa.eu/pub/pdf/other/virtualcurrencyschemesen.pdf [Accessed: 29th April 2015].

[46] Internet Document, Emily Spaven, "Isle of Man Introduces Regulation for Bitcoin Businesses", 2015 [Online]. Available: www.coindesk.com/isle-of-man-introduces-regulation-for-bitcoin-businesses [Accessed: 26th March 2015].

[47] Internet Document, Government of the Isle of Man, "Questions and Answers – Digital Currencies", 2014 [Online]. Available: www.gov.im/media/1197369/questions_and_answers_re_iom_position_on_digital_currencies_final.pdf [Accessed: 18th June 2014].

[48] Internet Document, Government of Singapore, "MAS to Regulate Virtual Currency Intermediaries for Money Laundering and Terrorist Financing Risks", 2014 [Online]. Available: www.mas.gov.sg/news-and-publications/media-releases/2014/mas-to-regulate-virtual-currency-intermediaries-for-money-laundering-and-terrorist-risks.aspx [Accessed: 14th March 2014].

[49] Internet Document, Pete Rizzo, "Bitcoin Regulation Remains on Agenda for California Agency" 2015 [Online]. Available: www.coindesk.com/bitcoin-regulation-remains-agenda-california-agency [Accessed: 23rd May 2015].

[50] Internet Document, Yessi Bello Perez, "North Carolina House Seeks Oversight of Bitcoin Activities", 2015 [Online]. Available: www.coindesk.com/north-carolina-representatives-pass-bitcoin-bill-by-wide-margin [Accessed: 22nd May 2015].

[51] Internet Document, Connecticut Legislature, "Substitute House Bill No. 6800", 2015 [Online]. Available: www.cga.ct.gov/2015/FC/2015HB-06800-R000177-FC.htm [Accessed: 22nd June 2015].

[52] Internet Document, No Author Given, "Connecticut Bill to Impose New Restrictions on Bitcoin MSBs", 2015 [Online]. Available: http://bitcoinvox.com/article/1672/connecticut-bill-to-restrict-bitcoin [Accessed: 22nd June 2015].

[53] Internet Document, State of Washington Department of Financial Institutions, "Bitcoin and Virtual Currency Regulation", 2015 [Online]. Available: www.dfi.wa.gov/bitcoin [Accessed: 19th June 2015].

[54] Internet Document, United States Department of the Treasury, "Financial Crimes Enforcement Network", 2015 [Online]. Available: www.fincen.gov [Accessed: 24th June 2015].

[55] Internet Document, United States Department of the Treasury, "Application of FinCEN Regulations to Presons Administering Exchanges or Using Virtual Currencies FIN-2013-G001", 2015 [Online]. Available: http://fincen.gov/statutes_regs/guidance/html/FIN-2013-G001.html [Accessed: 24 June 2015].

[56] Internet Document, United States Department of the Treasury, "Application of FinCEN Regulations to Virtual Currency Mining Operations FIN-2014-R001", 2015 [Online]. Available: www.fincen.gov/news_room/rp/rulgins/pdf/FIN-2014-R001.pdf [Accessed: 23rd June 2015].

[57] Internet Document, United States Department of the Treasury, "Application of Fin CEN Regulations to Virtual Currency Software Development and Certain Investment Activity FIN-2014-R002", 2015 [Online]. Available: www.fincen.gov/news_room/rp/rulings/pdf/FIN-2014-R002.pdf [Accessed: 23rd June 2015].

[58] Internet Document, United States Department of the Treasury, "Application of FinCEN Regulations to Virtual Currency Trading Platform FIN-2014-R011", 2015 [Online]. Available: www.fincen.gov/news_room/rp/rulings/pdf/FIN-2014-R011.pdf [Accessed: 24th June 2015].

[59] Internet Document, United States Department of the Treasury, "Application of FinCEN Regulations to Virtual Currency Payment System FIN-2014-R012", 2015 [Online]. Available: www.fincen.gov/news_room/rp/rulings/pdf/FIN-2014-R012.pdf [Accessed: 23rd June 2015].

[60] Internet Document, International Monetary Fund, "Financial Derivatives", 2015 [Online]. Available: www.imf.org/external/np/sta/fd [Accessed: 1st May 2015].

[61] Internet Document, No Author Given, "The Bitcoin Derivative Boom Can Be A Mark Of The Cryptocurrency's Coming Of Age", 2014 [Online]. Available: www.forbes.com/sites/ericxlmu/2014/08/07/the-bitcoin-derivative-boom-can-be-a-mark-of-the-coming-of-age-of-the-digital-currency [Accessed: 8th August 2014].

[62] Internet Document, Joon Ian Wong, "CFTC Chairman: We Have Oversight Of Bitcoin Derivatives", 2014 [Online]. Available: www.coindesk.com/cftc-chairman-oversight-bitcoin-derivatives [Accessed 11th December 2014].

[63] Internet Document, Commodities Futures Trading Commission, "Application for Registration as a Derivatives Clearing Organization for LedgerX LLC, a Proposed Bitcoin Derivatives Exchange and Clearing House", 2014 [Online]. Available: http://sirt.cftc.gov/sirt/sirt.aspx?Topic=ClearingOrganizationsAD&Key=30998 [Accessed 2nd February 2015].

[64] Internet Document, Commodities Futures Trading Commission, "LedgerX Swap Execution and Facility Application Documents", 2014 [Online]. Available: http://sirt.cftc.gov/SIRT/SIRT.aspx?Topic=SwapExecutionFacilitiesAD&Key=30643 [Accessed 23rd June 2015].

[65] Internet Document, TeraExchange, "TeraExchange", 2015 [Online]. Available www.teraexchange.com [Accessed: 7th June 2015].

[66] Internet Document, Zach Miners, "Swap agreement aims to protect Bitcoin holders from the next crash" 2015 [Online]. Available: www.pcworld.com/article/2111201/swap-agreement-aims-to-protect-bitcoin-holders-from-the-next-crash.html [Accessed: 30th May 2015].

[67] Internet Document, TeraExchange, "TeraExchange Rules and CFTC Submission", 2015 [Online]. Available: www.teraexchange.com/RND.html [Accessed: 23rd May 2015].

[68] Internet Document, Government of the Isle of Man, "Questions and Answers -- Digital Currencies", 2014 [Online]. Available: www.gov.im/media/1197368/questions_and_answers_re_iom_position_on_digital_currencies_final.pdf [Accessed: 18th June 2014].

[69] Internet Document, Pablo Fernandez Burgueno, "Twelve Things You Should Know Before Using Bitcoin", 2013 [Online]. Available: www.abanlex.com/index.php?s=bitcoin [Accessed: 5th January 2014].

[70] Internet Document, Kate Walsh and Jason Murphy, "ATO Targets Bitcoin Users", 2013 [Online]. Available: www.afr.com/p/technology/ato_targets_bitcoin_users_oawpzLQHDz2vEUWtvYLTWI [Accessed: 15th July 2013].

[71] Internet Document, Stan Higgins, "New York State Tax Agency: Bitcoin Buyers Don't Need to Pay Sales Tax", 2014 [Online]. Available: www.coindesk.com/new-york-sales-tax-agency-bitcoin-buyers-dont-need-pay-sales-tax [Accessed: 30th December 2014].

[72] Internet Document, United States Internal Revenue Service, "Intangibles", 2014 [Online]. Available: www.irs.gov/Businesses/Small-Businesses-&-Self-Employed/Intangibles [Accessed: 22nd May 2015].

[73] Internet Document, Kevin Johnston, "Taxes vs. Intangibles". 2014 [Online]. Available: http://smallbusiness.chron.com/taxes-us-intagibles-10577.html [Accessed: 25th May 2015].

[74] Internet Document, Joseph Henchman, Richard Borean, "States' Sales Taxes on Software", 2015 [Online]. Available: http://taxfoundation.org/blog/states-sales-taxes-software [Accessed: 22nd May 2015].

[75] Internet Document, Larry Loeb, "Chicago Cloud Computing Tax Is Not Amusing", 2015 [Online]. Available: www.informationweek.com/cloud/chicago-clpoud-computing-tax-us-not-amusing/a/d-id/1321187 [Accessed: 6th July 2015].

[76] Skatteverket v. David Hedqvist, European Court of Justice, Case C-264-14.

[77] Internet Document, Aoife White, "Bitcoin Tax-Free Transactions Face Test at Top EU Court", 2014 [Online]. Available: www.bloomberg.com/news/articles/2014-07-30/bitcoin-tax-free-transactions-face-test-at-top-eu-court [Accessed: 22nd May 2015].

[78] Internet Document, Alejandro Gomez de la Cruz, "Bitcoin is exempt from VAT in Spain", 2015 [Online]. Available: http://lawandbitcoin.com/en/bitcoin-is-vat-exempt-in-spain [Accessed: 22nd May 2015].

[79] Internet Document, Giulio Prisco, "Swiss Tax Authorities Confirm that Bitcoin is VAT-Free in Switzerland", 2015 [Online]. Available: http://bitcoinmagazine.com/20833/swiss-tax-authorities-confirm-bitcoin-vat-free-switxerland [Accessed: 20th June 2015].

[80] Internet Document, Norwegian Tax Authority, "Use of Bitcoins – Tax Issues", 2013 [Online]. Available: www.skatteetaten.no/no/Radgiver/Rettskilder/Uttalelser/Prinsipputtalelser/Bruk-av-bitcoins--Skatte--oq-avgiftsmessige-konsekvenser [Accessed: 11th November 2013].

[81] Internet Document, Yves Smith, "Is UCC Article 9 Going to Kill the Use of Bitcoin by US Businesses", 2015 [Online]. Available: www.nakedcapitalsim.com/2041/03/ucc-article-9-going-kill-us-bitcoin-us-businesses.html [Accessed: 14th May 2015].

[82] Internet Document, United States Internal Revenue Service, "IRS Virtual Currency Guidance: Virtual Currency is Treated as Property for Federal Tax Purposes; General Rules for Property Transactions Apply", 2014 [Online]. Available: www.irs.gov/uac/Newsroom/IRS-Virtual-Currency-Guidance [Accessed: 17th April 2014].

[83] Internet Document, Mike Ward, "What will be the impact of the US Government bitcoin sell-off?", 2014 [Online]. Available: https://bitscan.com/articles/what-will-be-the-impact-of-the-us-government-bitcoin-sell-off [Accessed: 1st May 2015].

[84] Internet Document, U.S. Department of Justice, "Auction Notice", 2014 [Online]. Available: www.usmarshals.gov/assets/2014/bitcoins [Accessed: 27th June 2014].

[85] Internet Document, Jon Matonis, "Government Sale of Bitcoin Established Fungibility Precedent", 2014 [Online]. Available: www.coindesk.com/government-asle-bitcoin-establishes-fungibility-precedent [Accessed: 27th June 2014].

[86] Internet Document, Robert McMillan, "The Inside Story of Mt. Gox, Bitcoin's $460 Million Disaster", 2014 [Online]. Available: www.wired.com/2014/03/bitcoin-exchange [Accessed: 31st May 2015].

[87] Internet Document, Jon Russell, "Mt. Gox Customers Can Now File Claims For Their Bitcoins", 2015 [Online]. Available: http://techcrunch.com/2015/04/22/mt-gox-claims and www.kraken.com [Accessed: 30th May 2015].

[88] Internet Document, Office of the United States Trade Representative, "Bilateral Investment Treaties", 2015 [Online]. Available: https://ustr.gov/trad-agreements/bilateral-investment-treaties [Accessed: 21st May 2015].

[89] Internet Document, United States Department of State, "Bilateral Investment Treaties", 2015 [Online]. Available: www.state.gov/e/eb/ifd/bit [Accessed: 21st May 2015].

[90] Internet Document, United States Department of State, "2012 U.S. Model BIT", 2015 [Online]. Available: www.state.gov/documents/organization/188371.pdf [Accessed: 21st May 2015].

[91] Internet Document, Cade Metz, "The Next Big Thing You Missed: There's a Sure-Fire Way to Control the Price of Bitcoin", 2014 [Online]. Available: www.wired.com/2014/01/bitcoin-derivative [Accessed: 22nd May 2015].

[92] Internet Document, Jared Paul Marx, "Token Sales and the US' Impressionistic Securities Laws", 2015 [Online]. Available: www.coindesk.com/token-sales-and-the-us-impressionistic-securities-laws [Accessed: 21st March 2015].

[93] Internet Document, Vero Skett, "Income Taxation of Virtual Currencies", 2013 [Online]. Available: www.vero.fi/sv-FI/Detaljerade_skatteanvisninqar/Inkomsttbeskattning_av_personkunder/Inkomstbeskattning_av_virtuella_valutor%2828454%29 [Accessed: 15th October 2013].

[94] Internet Document, Ela Levy-Weinrib, "Government Considers Taxing Bitcoin Profits", 2013 [Online]. Available: www.globes.co.is/serveen/globes/docreview.asp?did=1000879015 [Accessed: 1st October 2013].

[95] Internet Document, No Author Given, "Dail Debates 126", 2013 [Online]. Available: http://oireachtasdebates.oireachtas.ie/debates%20authoring/debateswebpack.nsf/takes/dail2013121000054?opendocument [Accessed: 15th December 2013].

[96] Internet Document, Jon Southurst, "Australian Regulator: Bitcoin is Not a Financial Product", 2014 [Online]. Available: www.coindesk.com/australian-regulator-bitcoin-financial-product [Accessed: 16th December 2014].

[97] Internet Document, John Kelleher, "Medici, The Bitcoin Stock Exchange", 2014 [Online]. Available: www.ubvestopedia.com/articles/investing/121014/medici-blockchain-stock-exchange.esp [Accessed: 20th December 2014].

[98] Internet Document, Stan Higgins, "SEC Filing Hints at Overstock's Plan for Bitcoin-Based Securities", 2014 [Online]. Available: www.coindesk.com/sec-filing-hints-at-overstocks-plan-for-bitcoin-based-securities [Accessed: 28th April 2015].

[99] Internet Document, Cade Metz, "Overstock's Radical Plan to Reinvent the Stock Market with Bitcoin", 2014 [Online]. Available: www.wired.com/2014/06/overstock-and-cryptocurrency [Accessed: 9th May 2015].

[100] Internet Document, Yessi Bello Perez, "Sweden's Nasdaq Exchange Approves Bitcoin-based ETN", 2015 [Online]. Available: www.coindesk.com/swedens-nasdaq-exchange-approves-bitcoin-based-etn [Accessed: 29th April 2015].

[101] Internet Document, Crypto:Stocks, "Crypto Stocks", 2015 [Online]. Available: https://cryptostocks.com [Accessed: 23rd May 2015].

[102] Internet Document, Finanstilsynet, "Warnings Against Digital Currencies", 2013 [Online]. Available: www.finanstilsynet.dk/da/Nyhedscenter/Pressemeddelelser/2013/Advarsel-mod-virtuelle-valutaer-bitcoin-mfl-2013.aspx [Accessed: 31st December 2013].

[103] Internet Document, Jon Southurst, "Australian Regulator: Bitcoin is Not a Financial Products", 2014 [Online]. Available: www.coindesk.com/austrlaian-regulator-bitcoin-financial-product [Accessed: 16th December 2014].

[104] SEC v. Shavers *et al.*, U.S. Dist. Ct. E. Dist. Texas, Case No. 4:13-CV-416; U.S. v. Shavers, U.S. Dist. Ct. S. Dist. N.Y., Case No. 14-mag-02465, and U.S. v. Shavers, *et al.*, U.S. Dist. Ct. E. Dist. Texas, Case No. 14-mj-00355

[105] INTERNET DOCUMENT, Jonathan Stempel, "Texan charged in first bitcoin securities fraud Ponzi case", 2015 [Online]. Available: www.reuters.com/warticle/2014/11/06/us-bitcoin-charges-idYSKBN0Q21120141106 [Accessed: 28th May 2015].

References

[106] Internet Document, Kathryn Kaoudis, "SEC v. Shavers: Over $40 Million Disgorged in Bitcoin Fraud Case", 2015 [Online]. Available: www.theracetothebottom.org/2015/2/25/sec-v-shavers-over-40-million-disgorged-in-bitcoin-fraud-cas.html [Accessed: 26th May 2015].

[107] Internet Document, U.S. Securities Exchange Commission, "SEC Alert", 2015 [Online]. Available: www.sec.gov/investor/alerts/ia_virtualcurrencies.pdf and Dara Kerr, "Bitcoin is ripe for fraud and Ponzi schemes, warns SEC", 2015 [Online]. Available: www.cnet.com/news/bitcoin-is-ripe-for-fraud-and-ponzi-schemes-warns-sec [Accessed: 27th May 2015].

[108] Internet Document, No Author Given, "China Police Detain Three in Bitcoin Fraud Case, Xinhua Says", 2013 [Online]. Available: www.bloomberg.com/news/articles/2013-12-04/china-police-detain-three-in-bitcoin-fraud-case-xinhua-says [Accessed: 14th December 2014].

[109] Internet Document, Overstock.com, Inc., "Form S-3 Securities Registration Statement", 2014 [Online]. Available: www.sec.gov/Archives/edgar/data/1130713/0000104746915003890/a2224281zs-3.htm [Accessed: 26th June 2015].

[110] Internet Document, Carlo Caraluzzo, "Patrick Byrne: Medici Will Be a National Market System Compliant and Able to Trade Everything", 2015 [Online]. Available: http://cointelegraph.com/news/113281/patrick-byrne-medici-will-be-a-national-market-system-compliant-and-able-to-trade-everything [Accessed: 25th June 2015].

[111] Internet Document, Joe Pugliese, "Overstock Files to Offer Stock That Works Like Bitcoin", 2015 [Online]. Available: www.wired.com/2015/04/overstock-files-offer-stock-works-like-bitcoin [Accessed: 26th June 2015].

[112] Internet Document, Pete Rizzo, "Overstock Invests in Broker-Dealer Ahead of Decentralized Stock Market Launch", 2015 [Online]. Available: www.coindesk.com/overstock-medici-pro-securities [Accessed: 26th June 2015].

[113] Internet Document, Pete Rizzo, "New York Reveals BitLicense Framework", 2014 [Online]. Available: www.coindesk.com/new-york-reveals-bitlicense-framework-bitcoin-businesses [Accessed: 14th October 2014].

[114] Internet Document, No Author Given, "New York State Department of Financial Services", 2014 [Online]. Available: www.scribd.com/doc/234246673/NEW-YORK-STATE-DEPARTMENT-OF-FINANCIAL-SERVICES-PROPOSED-NEW-YORK-CODES-RULES-AND-REGULATION [Accessed: 14th October 2014].

[115] Internet Document, New York Department of Financial Services, "Final NYDFS BitLicense Regulations", 2015 [Online]. Available: www.dfs.ny.gov/legal/regulations/adoptions/dfsp200t.pdf [Accessed: 24th June 2015].

[116] Internet Document, No Author Given, "California Bill Proposes License Requirement for Bitcoin Businesses", 2014 [Online]. Available: www.coindesk.com/california-bill-license-require-bitcoin-business [Accessed: 10th March 2015].

[117] Internet Document, Emily Spaven, "Accenture: UK Government Should Regulate Bitcoin Wallets", 2015 [Online]. Available: www.coindesk.com/accenture-uk-government-shoul-regulate-bitcoin-wallets [Accessed: 26th May 2015].

[118] Internet Document, Stan Higgins, "Canadian Senate Panel Calls for 'Light Touch' Bitcoin Regulation", 2015 [Online]. Available: www.coindesk.com/canadian-senate-panel-calls-for-light-touch-bitcoin-regulation [Accessed: 22nd June 2015].

[119] Internet Document, No Author Given, "Wanted: Replacement for (the Now Closed) ClearCoin Escrow", 2015 [Online]. Available: http://bitcoinmoney.com/post/6920197867/clearcoin-closes [Accessed: 29th May 2015].

[120] Internet Document, No Author Given, "The Next Level of Bitcoin Consumer Protection Revealed: Bitrated Introduces an Online Reputation Management and Payment System for Bitcoin Users", 2015 [Online]. Available: www.pcnewswire.com/news-releases/the-next-level-of-bitcoin-consumer-protection-revealed-bitrated-introduces-an-online-repitation-management-and-ayment-system-for-bitcoin-users-292390651.html [Accessed: 16th June 2015].

[121] Internet Document, John Villasenor, "Could 'Multisig' Help Bring Consumer Protection to Bitcoin Transactions?", 2015 [Online]. Available: www.forbes.com/sites/johnvillasenor/2014/03/28/could-multisig-help-bring-consumer-protection-to-bitcoin-trnsactions [Accessed: 12th June 2015].

[122] Internet Document, Nathaniel Popper, "In the Murky World of Bitcoin, Fraud is Quicker Than the Law", 2013 [Online]. Available: http://dealbook.nytimes.com/2013/12/05/in-the-murky-world-of-bitcoin-fraud-is-quicker-than-the-law [Accessed: 28th May 2015].

[123] Internet Document, Rupert Jones, "Paypal washes its hands of bitcoin scam", 2014 [Online]. Available: www.theguardian.com/money/2014/mar/01/paypal-bitcoin-scam-ebay [Accessed: 29th May, 2015].

[124] Internet Document, U.S. Federal Bureau of Investigation, "Former Federal Agents Charged with Bitcoin Money Laundering and Wire Fraud Agents were Part of Baltimore's Silk Road Task Force", 2015 [Online]. Available: www.fbi.gov/sanfrancisco/press-releases/2015/former-federal-agents-charged-with-bitcoin-money-laundering-and-wire-fraud [Accessed: 27th May 2015].

[125] Internet Document, Bitcoin Association of Hong Kong, "Statement on Recent Fraud Cases", 2015 [Online]. Available: www.bitcoinhk.org/2015-statement-on-recent-fraud-cases [Accessed: 27th May 2015].

[126] Internet Document, Reserve Bank of India, "RBI Cautions Users of Virtual Currencies Against Risks", 2013 [Online]. Available: http://rbi.org.in/scripts/BS_PressReleaseDisplay.aspx?prid=30247 [Accessed: 2nd January 2014].

[127] Internet Document, Robert McMillan, "The Inside Story of Mt. Gox, Bitcoin's $460 Million Disaster", 2015 [Online]. Available: www.wired.com/2014/03/bitcoin-exchange [Accessed: 31st May 2015].

[128] Internet Document, Zack Whittaker, "Bitstamp exchange hacked $5M worth of bitcoin stolen", 2015 [Online]. Available: www.zdnet.com/article/bitstamp-exchange-syspended-amid-hack-concerns-heres-what-we-know [Accessed: 29th May 2015].

[129] Internet Document, Eric Barber, "Insurance Coverage Available for Bitcoin Deposits – Devil is in the Details", 2015 [Online]. Available: www.virtualcurrencyreport.com/2014/01/insurance-coverage-available-for-bitcoin-deposits-devil-is-in-the-details [Accessed: 25th May 2015].

[130] Internet Document, Xapo, "Xapo Terms of Use", 2015 [Online]. Available: https://xapo.com/terms [Accessed: 31st May 2015].

[131] Internet Document, New York Conference of State Bank Supervisors, "State Regulatory Requirements for Virtual Currency Activities CSBS Draft Model Regulatory Framework and Request for Public Comment", 2014 [Online]. Available: www.csbs.org/regulatory/ep/Documents/CSBSDraftModelRegulatoryFrameworkforVirtualCurrencyProposal--Dec.162014.pdf [Accessed: 20th December 2014].

[132] Internet Document, Mike Orcutt, "Why Bitcoin Could Be Much More Than a Currency", 2015 [Online]. Available: www.technologyreview.com/news/537246/why-bitcoin-could-be-much-more-than-a-currency [Accessed: 9th May 2015].

[133] Internet Document, Primavera De Filippi, "Tomorrow's Apps Will Come From Brilliant (And Risky) Bitcoin Code", 2014 [Online]. Available: www.wired.com/2014/03/decentralized-applications-built-bitcoin-great-except-whos-responsible-outcomes [Accessed: 30th March 2014].

[134] Internet Document, No Author Given, "Bitmessage", 2015 [Online]. Available: www.reddit.com/bitmessage [Accessed: 10th January 2015].

[135] Internet Document, No Author Given, "Namecoin", 2015 [Online]. Available: https://namecoin.info [Accessed: 2nd February 2015].

[136] Internet Document, No Author Given, "Ethereum", 2015 [Online]. Available: https://www.ethereum.org [Accessed: 5th March 2015].

[137] Internet Document, No Author Given, "Counterparty", 2015 [Online]. Available: http://counterparty.io [Accessed: 9th May 2015].

[138] Internet Document, No Author Given, "Factom", 2015 [Online]. Available: http://factom.org [Accessed: 9th May 2015].

[139] Internet Document, Bitcoin, "Legal Disclaimer" 2015 [Online]. Available: https://bitcoin.org/en/legal [Accessed: 14th May 2015].

[140] Internet Document, TeraExchange, "TeraExchange Rulebook", 2015 [Online]. Available: www.teraexchange.com/RND.html [Accessed: 1st June 2015].

[141] Internet Document, Flexcoin, "Terms of Service", 2015 [Online]. Available: http://flexcoin.com/118.html [Accessed: 6th June 2015].

[142] Internet Document, Bitcoin, "Legal Disclaimer", 2015 [Online]. Available: https://bitcoin.org/en/legal [Accessed: 14th May 2015].

[143] Internet Document, Kraken, "Terms of Service", 2015 [Online]. Available: www.kraken.com/en-us/legal/tos [Accessed: 1st June 2015].

[144] Internet Document, Coinbase, "User Agreement", 2015 [Online]. Available: www.coinbase.com/legal/user_agreement [Accessed: 2nd June 2015].

[145] Internet Document, U.S. Federal Trade Commission, "Bitcoins", 2015 [Online]. Available: www.consumer.ftc.gov/blog/paying-bitcoins [Accessed: 26th June 2015].

[146] Internet Document, Pete Rizzo, "FTC Warns Consumers of Bitcoin Shopping Risks", 2015 [Online]. Available: www.coindesk.com/ftc-warns-consumers-bitcoin-shopping-risks [Accessed: 28th June 2015].

[147] Internet Document, U.S. Federal Trade Commission, "At FTC's Request, Court Halts Bogus Bitcoin Mining Operation", 2015 [Online]. Available: www.ftc.gov/news-events/press-releases/2014/09/ftcs-request-court-halts-bogus-bitcoin-mining-operation [Accessed: 24th June 2015].

[148] Internet Document, U.S. Consumer Financial Protection Bureau, "Risks to consumers posed by virtual currencies", 2015 [Online]. Available: http://files.consumerfinance.gov/f/201408_cfpb_consumer-advisory_virtual_currencies.pdf [Accessed: 16th June 2015].

[149] Internet Document, U.S. Consumer Financial Protection Bureau, "Regulation E Proposed Rule", 2015 [Online]. Available: www.consumerfinance.gov/newsroom/cfpb-proposes-strong-federal-protections-for-prepaid-products [Accessed: 22nd June 2015].

[150] Internet Document, U.S. Consumer Financial Protection Bureau, "Submit a complaint", 2015 [Online]. Available: www.consumerfianance.gov/complaint [Accessed: 23rd June 2015].

[151] Internet Document, U. S. Congress, "U.S. Computer Fraud and Abuse Act", 18 U.S.C. Code Sect. 1030, 2015 [Online]. Available: www.law.cornell.edu/uscode/18/1030.html [Accessed: 23rd June 2015].

Subject Index

Subject Index

A

Aldernay (Channel Islands) 7
antitrust 86, 87
arbitration 93
auction 54
Australia 49, 68, 72

B

bankruptcy 54, 55
Belgium 7, 52
Bilateral Investment Treaties 55, 56
Bitcoin 3, 4, 5, 6, 7, 9, 10, 14, 15, 20, 22, 23, 24, 25, 29, 30, 31, 39, 42, 45, 47, 52, 54, 55, 68, 70, 87, 88, 89, 94
BitLicense 78
Bitmessage 88
Bitstamp 83, 84
blockchain 4, 5, 31, 32, 33
Bolivia 25
Brazil 7, 8, 27, 81
Butterfly Labs 96, 97

C

California 41, 72, 78
Canada 19, 33, 55, 79
Chicago 51
China 9, 25, 74, 83
Coinbase 93
Commodities Futures Trading Commission 46, 47, 60, 64
commodities trading exchange 10, 47
commodity 30, 45, 46, 47, 59, 60, 63, 64
complaints 97, 98
Computer Fraud and Abuse Act 98
Connecticut 41
Consumer Financial Protection Bureau 97, 98
consumer protection 10, 85, 95, 96
contracts 10, 88, 89, 90, 91, 92
Counterparty 88, 89
creditor 53
criminal law 10
Croatia 23
crypto-stocks 69
currency 13, 29, 34, 35
cyber-securities 69
Cyprus 26

D

Denmark 72

Department of Justice 54
Department of the Treasury 42, 44
derivatives 46, 63
digital currency 3, 7, 10, 11, 12, 13, 17, 18, 22, 27, 28, 30, 45, 46
dirty money 36
disclaimer 91, 92

E

Ecuador 20, 21, 22, 31
Electronic Currency System 20
escrow services 79, 80
Estonia 52
Ethereum 88, 90
European Community 31
European Court of Justice 52
European Union 28
exchanges 6, 27

F

Factom 89
Federal Trade Commission 85, 95, 96
fiat currency 14, 15
fiduciary currency 14
Financial Crimes Enforcement Network (FinCEN) 42, 43, 44
financial instruments 70, 72
financial services 72
Finland 52, 67
foreign investments 55, 56, 57
France 19, 27, 28, 52
fraud 81, 82, 83
futures contract 46, 47

G

Germany 22, 23, 52
Greece 31

H

Hawaii 51

I

Iceland 24
India 23
Indonesia 19
insurance 84, 85
intangible assets 50
Internal Revenue Service 50, 54

Ireland 68
Isle of Man 31, 32, 33, 34, 38, 48
Israel 68
itBit 30

K
Kenya 34
know your customer requirement 39
Kraken 93
Kyrgyzstan 26

L
LedgerX 47, 60, 64
legal tender 13, 17
liability limits 91, 92, 93
lien 52, 53
Luxembourg 27

M
Malta 28
Mexico 21
mining 5, 6, 83
money laundering 9, 37, 38, 39, 40,41, 42, 43, 44
Money Services Businesses 42, 43
money transfer 41
money transmission 9, 41, 44
M-Pesa 34
Mt. Gox 55, 83, 84
Multisig 80

N
Namecoin 88
Netherlands 19
New Mexico 51
New York 30, 49, 72, 77, 78, 86
New Zealand 14
Nigeria 34
North Carolina 41
Norway 52

O
OKCoin 47
Overstock.com 68, 69, 74, 75

P
PayPal 82
Poland 52
Ponzi scheme 73
private money 15, 17
Project Medici 68, 69
property 47, 48, 50, 53-55, 57

R
risk 19, 20, 94
Russia 25, 26

S
sales tax 48, 49, 50, 51
securities 65, 67, 76
Securities and Exchange Commission 69, 71, 73, 75
securities exchange 69, 74, 75
securities trading 74, 75
security interest 53
Shavers Case 73
Silk Road 54, 82
Singapore 20, 40, 41
smart contracts 88, 89, 90, 91
South Dakota 51
Spain 48
Sweden 52, 69
Switzerland 52

T
tax 48, 49, 50, 68
Tennessee 51
TeraExchange 47, 60, 64, 92
Texas 51
Thailand 24, 25
theft 83, 84
trade agreements 56
trading exchange 6, 60
trusted platforms 80, 81
Turkey 14, 55

U
Uniform Commercial Code 53
United Kingdom 78, 82
use tax 51

V
value added tax 48, 52
Vietnam 25
virtual currency 6, 9, 10, 11, 17, 21, 22, 24, 25, 26, 29, 30, 34, 70

W
wallets 3, 4, 6, 28, 79
Washington 42

X
Xapo 84

Made in the USA
Lexington, KY
07 September 2018